Hey God, Can We Talk?

Hey God, Can We Talk?

Conversations With God
by H.S.

XULON PRESS

Xulon Press
2301 Lucien Way #415
Maitland, FL 32751
407.339.4217
www.xulonpress.com

Paperback ISBN-13: 978-1-66283-504-9
Ebook ISBN-13: 978-1-66283-505-6

This book is dedicated to YOU.
God said you are important to Him.
He loves you. He wants to sit down
besides you and talk and listen to you.

Acknowledgments

Thank you, Lord, for guiding me and allowing me to be your vessel. I thank you and praise you for telling me to share everything with my dear friend, L.M.

I'm eternally grateful to L.M. She devoted countless hours to reading my drafts despite her busy schedule. She provided me with the insights I needed. She gave me encouragement when I was discouraged. Even though we are miles apart, I felt she was right beside me on this new journey. God knew she was the perfect person to help me! She touched my life and soul!

Thank you to my husband and all of my children. My husband unconditionally loves me and lets me be me! I'm so touched that he prays for me every day. Thank you to my children for their endless support and especially their feedback, since I constantly bugged them. They gave me valuable input! Thank you to one of my daughters (C.I.L.) for writing a heartfelt note to include in the book. Her words brought tears to my eyes and touched my soul. I am grateful to another daughter (C.E.) for capturing the essence of this book by writing a summary for the back of the book.

A very special thank you to my amazing parents. Both of them are godly examples of God's Love! My dad has a heart of gold for everyone; while my mom has the best listening ear and always sees the best in everyone, especially me.

Thank you to A.E. for being a generous editor and a humble servant of God.

God sent T.S. at the right time. I'm thankful for her assistance in creating the book design.

Thank you to B.K., D.S. and K.D. for reading each of the entries and for the book reviews you each took time to write. Your words touched my heart and helped me continue on this path God put me on.

And finally, to ALL the wonderful friends and family that have read these devotions and provided feedback to me along this journey. Their comments uplifted me because they knew I was hesitant and scared of taking on this challenge that was new to me. I'm thankful for their encouragement and honesty.

God blessed me with them! I am forever grateful to all of you!

Note from Author's Daughter

If you've picked up this book, please know that someone really cares about you. H.S., the author, spent a ton of time having these conversations with God, and then dutifully documented them. She, herself, will tell you that she is not a writer, so please understand that this was a labor of love and obedience. As you dig into the devotional, you'll learn that H.S. is a not-so-secret rebel at heart so you should really appreciate the "obedience" part. These conversations are the kind that you would have with an old friend, a partner, or a confidante, so be prepared for the vulnerability and the honesty that comes along with those types of relationships.

Before you venture any further, I thought it would also be helpful for you to understand a little about H.S. so that you can know how she comes to this venture in her life. She is the kind of person who you call when you feel like the world is falling down around you, knowing that she will be there to pick you up with prayer and kindness. She will laugh with you, cry with you, be angry over the injustice of it all, and still she will be truly authentic in her love of Christ. She is a pillar of faith, and an example of what God hopes for in a Christian. She is protective, she is hopeful, and she will always look for the good in people. As you spend time with this devotional, you will see what an honest relationship with God can look like because she has been authentic in her descriptions. You will be a part of the small moments that she has shared with God, and hopefully you will see that God is approachable in addition to benevolent. H.S. has always spoken of her relationship with God in this way, and I am glad that she has finally had the time to share her very special friendship with you.

As a final thought, before I leave you to dig into the good stuff, I hope that you find this devotional to be comforting, to be fulfilling, and that it helps you to recognize that God is not a million miles away. I hope that you let H.S. open your heart to see that God can be right beside you. She is a formidable woman, who's prayers have always been a source of love and promise. And I am glad that you will get to know her through her conversations with God, and that you will feel the love that she has put into this. As her daughter, I have had many years to look to her as an example of a faithful believer and I am extremely proud of her dedication to doing God's work.

Table of Contents

Introduction

Hey God,

A few days ago, you were telling me to write a devotional book. But you know I don't like writing. I can't write beautifully like the devotional books I've read. That's not me! So, I don't understand why you want me to write one.

I understand your concerns and why you're questioning me. I know you don't feel comfortable writing, but you love talking with me. We have conversations all the time!

Yes, I love talking with you, Lord. You created me like that!

Yes, I gave you the gift of talking. I want you to write a different type of devotional book. I want it to be a collection of our conversations. I want people to know that spending time with me is just talking with a friend. I don't want you to write paragraphs with beautifully crafted words. I just want you to write our conversations down. Conversations are natural and more intimate.

I understand, but...

I know you're hesitant and a bit scared, but I'm here. I'll help you write the devotions. I don't want *you* to write them; the Holy Spirit will guide you. He'll tell you which conversations to write down— the ones others need to hear.

Hmmm. You're right about some of our conversations. They are amazing! Your lessons have opened my eyes and heart. You've touched my soul, and we've wept together!

Now, you understand me more. You're putting yourself aside. Now you're listening with an open heart. I'm pleased with your attitude now.

Okay, Lord, but how do I do this? How many do I write?

I want you to write fifty devotions or conversations.

Fifty? Are you crazy?

Don't you trust me?

Yeah, I guess. But fifty!

I want you to reread some of your journal entries for our conversations. Then I'll show you which ones to share.

You want me to reread my journals? How far back do you want me to go?

I want you to reread them starting from 2017—three years.

Do you want me to read three years' worth of my past journals? Lord, I already feel tired just thinking about it.

I will give you the strength to do this, so don't worry about anything. You'll enjoy rereading your journals. I also want you to share the conversations that we have throughout the day—not just when your Bible is open. I want everyone to know that I'm here all the time for them. I see and understand what's going on every minute.

Some people hear other Christians pray in a group. Those prayers are so eloquent, powerful, and beautifully crafted for me to hear. There's nothing wrong with that, but many feel inferior when they hear those prayers. They think they can't do that, so they hesitate to pray or talk to me.

Yeah, I used to feel like that too. But when I was a teenager, you told me to just be me and talk to you like a friend having a conversation. Why should I rehearse or plan what I'm going to say to you? I don't do that with my friends.

That's what I'm trying to say. So when you come before me, just tell me what you're thinking in your own words. I'm always here for you as a father is here for a child. I love you!

I know you love me. However, I think some people fear you because you're God! They don't want to talk to you.

I understand what you're saying. That's why I want others to hear our conversations. I don't want them to fear me. I want them to understand how much I love them. I know you're scared about writing this because you've never done anything like this before, but trust me. I'm putting you on a new journey that will touch many lives. I know your inner thoughts and prayers. More than anything, you want everyone to really get to know me and have a relationship with me. That's why I'm asking you to do this. Because I see your pure heart, and I see your tears flow when you think of others. This pleases me and touches my heart. So, let's do this together. I will continuously guide you. You just need to listen to me as you write.

Oh, yes, Lord. My tears are flowing as I write this. I want everyone to know you intimately as I do! Even though I'm nervous, scared, and don't feel confident in my writing skills, I will be obedient and listen and write.

You are my precious girl with a heart overflowing with love for others. When you were a young woman, you learned that I gave you the gift of evangelism. You weren't sure about it, so I had a good friend explain to you that you don't have to be like Billy Graham and be a preacher. Instead, just share the gospel with the people you meet. That gift of evangelism has given you a boldness to speak the truth. Throughout your life, you haven't been afraid to share God

with people you care about. But now it's time to share my love with the multitudes.

Yes, I understand, Lord. Thank you for reminding me about your gift of evangelism you gave me. You want me to take my sharing to the next level. Okay, Lord. Let's do this!

Yes, let's work together and start this new journey. Do you remember what I revealed to you about Peter?

Oh yes, I remember reading about Peter. I love that man because he's similar to me. He's strong, impulsive, and has a big mouth that gets him into trouble sometimes, but he loves you, Lord. When I was reading about him, that was the moment I felt the Spirit touch my soul and tell me that others need to hear about it.

Yes, my precious child. That's when this journey started. I planted a seed into your heart and mind. So, tell everyone about Peter. They're eager to know what you learned from him.

Okay, Lord. Then that's the first conversation I will write about.

Great! Now let's tell them about Peter!

Peter

"When they came back from the tomb, they told all these things to the Eleven and to all the others. It was Mary Magdalene, Joanna, Mary, the mother of James, and the others with them who told this to the apostles. But they did not believe the women because their words seemed to them like nonsense. Peter, however, got up and ran to the tomb. Bending over, he saw the strips of linen lying by themselves, and he went away, wondering to himself what had happened" (Luke 24:9-12, NIV).

I've read this before, Lord. Can you show me something *new*?

Of course, I can show you something you haven't seen before. Please reread it, but read it slowly. I want you to stop and picture what's happening, then think about the characters' feelings and what they're going through.

Okay.

"...they told all these things to the eleven and to all the others...but they did not believe the women..." (vv. 9, 11).

Lord, I know this is negative, but when I reread that part, all I could think about was "Men. Typical men! They don't believe what the women said!" If another woman heard them, she would have asked them more questions and then believed them! Sorry, God. It just upsets me the way some men treat women sometimes because it still happens today.

I understand how you feel. However, keep reading because one of the men was listening and wondering.

1

Okay.

> *"Peter, however, got up and ran to the tomb."*

Lord, I'm so glad Peter is wondering! Hurray for Peter!

Yes, I'm proud of Peter too! Do you remember what Peter did before I died?

Yes, he denied knowing you three times! That sucks, Lord! He's known for denying you. Poor Peter; pastors always preach about him.

Yes, he is known for that, but I'm going to show you something else he *should be* known for. At that time, he felt so ashamed. He had his doubts about everything that just happened. But he loved me so much that it hurt him immensely when he saw me die on the cross. He couldn't bear the pain!

I understand, Lord. When we love so much, the pain is more intense! You love him too! Peter was like one of the top three disciples that went with you to particular places. You asked him to sit and pray for you while you were in the Garden of Gethsemane. You took him, John, and James to the mountain top where he heard God say, *"This is my Son, whom I love; with him, I am well pleased. Listen to him!"* (Matthew 17:5, NIV).

Yes, I love Peter very much! But reread that part about Peter again, and read it slowly.

Okay, Lord.

> *"Peter, however, got up and ran to the tomb"* (Luke 24:12a).

He probably didn't believe the women either.

Yes, he wasn't sure about what the women said, but look at what he did. He *"got up and ran to the tomb."* Why did he go if he is questioning what the women said? The other men felt the women's words were nonsense.

Peter went to check it out for himself because he loved you so much. I think part of him is wondering and hoping that what the women said is true. He was holding on to a miracle.

Yes, Peter is wondering and trying to remember what I said to him before. I told the disciples that I would be raised from the dead, but they didn't understand me at that time. So, Peter went to see, even though he doubted.

The verse says, *"Peter, however, got up and <u>ran</u> to the tomb"* (Luke 24:12a, emphasis added). He ran, Lord! I love that! I see him running with tears in his eyes!

What does that also tell you about Peter?

Peter ran because this was so important to him. It's urgent! He needs to know now if Jesus is alive! He loves you so much, Lord!

Yes, he is running because he loves me. But I want you to stop and listen to me closely. I want you to breathe in and out slowly because you're full of emotions right now. You're having feelings like Peter. As Peter is running toward *me*, you are running too with tears in your heart. I want you to calm down a bit because I have something important to tell you.

Yes, Lord, you know me so well. I need to stop the tears and listen to you. Okay, I'm calm.

You're like Peter. You're strong and bold like him, but you have your doubts like he did. Lately, I've been telling you to do things out of

your comfort zone, and you're doubting too. However, what has been your response?

I've been trying to go forward, a little at a time, even though I have doubts. You've been making me do and say things I'm not used to. For example, you told me to pray for my nephew, so I sent him a prayer through the phone. I was shocked when he called to thank me because he definitely needed prayers. He thought his mom called me to tell me what was happening, but she didn't. You told me. Thank you, Lord, that I can be your vessel of love and encouragement to my nephew.

I'm pleased with your obedience because I know it's hard for you to obey, especially when you don't see the results right away. It's okay to doubt. Peter did too. But he still went forward. So, like Peter, I want you to continue to do things, even if you have doubts.

Okay, Lord.

Here's a phrase I want you to remember. This is what Peter *should be* known for: "Doubt but DO!"

> *"Trust in the LORD with all your heart and lean not on your own understanding; in all your ways, submit to him, and he will make your paths straight"* (Proverbs 3:5-6, NIV).

Reflections:

- What are you not doing because you have doubts?
- Why are you doubting God?
- What little steps can you take to go forward with God?
- Can you remember a time when you were filled with so much emotion that it made it difficult to hear from God?

Joseph

This is how the birth of Jesus the Messiah came about: His mother Mary was pledged to be married to Joseph, but before they came together, she was found to be pregnant through the Holy Spirit. Because Joseph, her husband, was faithful to the law, and yet did not want to expose her to public disgrace, he had in mind to divorce her quietly. But after he had considered this, an angel of the Lord appeared to him in a dream and said, "Joseph son of David, do not be afraid to take Mary home as your wife, because what is conceived in her is from the Holy Spirit. She will give birth to a son, and you are to give him the name Jesus, because he will save his people from their sins." All this took place to fulfill what the Lord had said through the prophet: "The virgin will conceive and give birth to a son, and they will call him Immanuel" (which means "God with us"). When Joseph woke up, he did what the angel of the Lord had commanded him and took Mary home as his wife. But he did not consummate their marriage until she gave birth to a son. And he gave him the name Jesus. (Matthew 1:18-25, NIV)

When they had gone, an angel of the Lord appeared to Joseph in a dream. "Get up," he said, "take the child and his mother and escape to Egypt. Stay there until I tell you, for Herod is going to search for the child to kill him." So he got up, took the child and his mother during the night and left for Egypt, where he stayed until the death of Herod. And so was fulfilled what the Lord had said through the prophet: "Out of Egypt, I called my son." After Herod died, an angel of the Lord appeared in a dream to Joseph in Egypt and said, "Get up, take the child and his mother and go to the land of Israel, for those who were trying to take the child's life are dead." So he got up, took the child and his mother, and went to the land of Israel. But when he heard that Archelaus was reigning in Judea in place of his father Herod, he was afraid to go there. Having been warned in a dream, he withdrew to the district of Galilee, and he went and lived in a town called Nazareth. So was fulfilled what was said through the prophets, that he would be called a Nazarene. (Matthew 2:13-14; 19-23, NIV)

What are these verses about?

They're about Joseph! We always hear about how wonderful Mary is, such a humble and obedient servant of God. But here, I see several incidents of the Holy Spirit speaking to Joseph! What a good daddy! He was an obedient servant to you, too!

Yes, Joseph was a good man! That's why I entrusted Jesus with Joseph and Mary. When Joseph found out about her being pregnant, what did he do?

He decided to divorce her quietly.

What does that tell you about Joseph?

He was an honorable man. He didn't want to hurt or disgrace Mary.

I can understand why you said that because you've heard other pastors say it. Why didn't he just marry her anyway?

Maybe he was a little scared.

Yes! He was hiding behind honor. He was a little scared of the situation. That's why I sent an angel to him in a dream. I made him confront his fear and reassured him that everything would work out.

That's why you said, *"Do not be afraid to take Mary home as your wife"* (Matthew 1:20, emphasis added). You knew he needed reassurance. You know us so well!

I made him confront his fear and deal with it with me. Only then would he learn to trust and believe me to help him through his fears. I kept sending angels to guide him.

Yes, you did! I loved it when Joseph *woke* up, *got* up, and *did* what the angel of the Lord commanded him! What great faith! I have respect for him as a man of God. Help me to be like Joseph. I want to listen and obey your instructions without questioning or doubting you. Lord, I feel I'm supposed to learn more, but I don't see it or hear it. Yet I sense you're tugging at my heart, telling me there's more but not yet.

(So tomorrow came, and we continued our conversation.)

I want you to reread the verses. You said you really liked how Joseph got up and did what the angel of the Lord commanded.

Yeah! I want to be like Joseph.

I understand because Joseph seems faithful, but do you know why he listened and obeyed without doubting?

Because he was your obedient servant?

Yes, but no. Joseph didn't come to me like that at first. Reread verses 19 and 20 from Chapter 1.

> *"Because Joseph, her husband, was faithful to the law, and yet did not want to expose her to public disgrace, he had in mind to divorce her quietly. But after he had considered this, an angel of the Lord appeared to him in a dream and said, 'Joseph son of David, do not be afraid to take Mary home as your wife, because what is conceived in her is from the Holy Spirit'"* (Matthew 1:19-20).

What was Joseph's first reaction to Mary's situation?

Like I said before, Joseph was planning on divorcing her quietly.

He thought about the problem and decided to handle the situation on his own without asking me. He rationalized various options and decided on his plan to resolve his embarrassment or shame by divorcing Mary quietly. That's how he felt. So he was going to divorce her quietly to protect himself too.

I understand why he handled the situation on his own because I tend to do this too. Instead of consulting you for wisdom, I rationalize, make excuses, and problem-solve to stop the pain or deal with a problem.

I'm glad you are understanding. Joseph needed to confront his fear instead of covering it up. I wanted Joseph to *stop and face his fear*! Verse 20 says, "... *do not be afraid to take Mary home as your wife...*"

The Bible doesn't explain everything in detail. While Joseph had his dream, I was making him face his fear. That meant being honest with his feelings of shame, anger, and doubt. Joseph needed to understand that *he had to accept* what was happening, and *he needed to make some changes*. Once he understood that and faced it, he humbly came before me with tears overflowing.

I get it, Lord. I want to grumble or blame others for my situation. But the problem is how I'm *responding* to the situation. I have a choice. Am I going to let the problem control me, or am I going to seek your wisdom? I need to make some changes in me, but that's hard to do, Lord.

I know it's hard for you. It was difficult for Joseph too. However, after Joseph understood that, he needed to make some changes in him. He was *free* to believe and trust me! He was open to being what I wanted him to be—a great daddy who listens and obeys me. Joseph needed this since he was in charge of taking care of my Son, Jesus!

I have an excellent plan for your life too. You have many more years ahead of you. So, relax and let go of your control and worries. Then you'll be *free* to believe in me, and you'll see amazing things!

Thank you, Lord. This is what you wanted to tell me! But why didn't you tell me yesterday?

I could have told you, but there was another lesson to learn. Yesterday I placed that unsettling feeling inside of you. I'm glad you listened and stopped, and we revisited the verses again. You could've just dismissed it, but you didn't. I'm pleased with you.

I'm trying to be your humble servant.

When you write about this conversation, don't forget to include the part of feeling a bit unsettled and there was a tugging at your heart.

Okay, Lord, but why?

Sometimes when we talk, you don't understand some things instantly. Sometimes the wisdom I'm giving you takes time. It may be a day or more, but you keep listening. There are times when I tell you to wait for the answer. I know you don't like to wait, and it makes you anxious. But continue to wait, and you'll see amazing things ahead!

Okay, but help me to wait. Please give me hope and encouragement, so I can keep going forward and wait upon you, Lord.

I also want to remember Joseph and what he did. First, he humbled himself and faced his fear. Then he confessed his sin, wept over it, and turned from his sin. Finally, he acknowledged you, Lord, and sought your wisdom instead of relying on himself. This is what I need to do too.

Reflections:

- What fear do you need to face?
- What are you grumbling about or blaming others for?
- You have a choice. Are you asking God for wisdom, or are you attempting to solve your problems or doing nothing?

The Sheep Will Scatter, But I Love Them

Then Jesus told them, "This very night you will all fall away on account of me, for it is written:

"'I will strike the shepherd, and the sheep of the flock will be scattered.'

But after I have risen, I will go ahead of you into Galilee."

Peter replied, "Even if all fall away on account of you, I never will."

"Truly I tell you," Jesus answered, "this very night, before the rooster crows, you will disown me three times."

But Peter declared, "Even if I have to die with you, I will never disown you." And all the other disciples said the same. (Matthew 26:31-35, NIV)

Jesus tells them they will all fall away by leaving him! Why did he tell them this? It's like telling me I'm going to fail.

I told them about what was going to happen to show them, my love.

Huh? You wanted to show them that you know everything that's going to happen, and that's a sign of your love for them?

You say that with a slight attitude, but I didn't say it like that. I knew everything that was going to happen. I said everything in love. Look at verse 32 again, *"But after I have risen, I will go ahead of you into Galilee."* I told them that everything would be fine even though

they would be scattered like a flock and run away. See the words, *"go ahead of you"*? Do you see that I wanted to see them again? I knew I would because I love them!

Yeah...You were trying to tell the disciples you will always love them, want to see them, even though you knew they would leave you. I get it now. You were also telling them that you will be alive again!

I love them despite their mistakes or what they consider their weaknesses. I will always love them. This is because they are so special to me.

I love you, too, no matter what. I see and know everything that's happening with you. But I will always love you because you are my precious child. Like you will always love your dear children no matter what happens.

Oh Lord, thank you for your overwhelming LOVE!

Reflections:

- Like the disciples, have you fled from God? If you have, he loves you no matter what you've done! So go back to him now.
- How would you react if Jesus told you that you were about to walk away from him? Would you be so focused on what he just said that you wouldn't be able to hear what He wants you to listen to?
- Reread verse 32. "'But after I have risen, I will go ahead of you into Galilee'" (emphasis added). God knows where you will be when you go astray. He's waiting for you. He loves you! Go to Him.

Quarantine Selfishness

Hey God,

This sucks! I don't like being sick with a bad case of bronchitis. It's been four weeks, Lord! Life isn't typical because my grandson and daughter aren't coming over here. Life wasn't that different when we had the "shelter in place" mandate for the pandemic. Things weren't that different because they had been coming over since I babysit him. Now they're not because I don't want them to get sick. I understand being in quarantine, but I didn't understand its impact on others because my life and routines didn't change that much. My husband and son went to work because they're considered "essential workers." However, *now* I understand a little bit about how others feel about being in quarantine. Forgive me, Lord, for being so ignorant to what others are feeling now.

I realize that I get annoyed faster when I do things for other people. I'm becoming lazy because I rest and watch too much TV. I feel like I don't have as much energy as before. I'm frustrated because I'm usually a high-energy person. Being isolated and alone is starting to irritate me!

I understand your frustration because you don't like the changes that are happening. However, you are upset with yourself. You didn't think that being sick for so long would create negative feelings and bring out your selfishness. Instead, you're only thinking about yourself and what you want, which is making you angry inside. You don't like how you're responding to everything that's been happening to you.

Yes, I hate this! I don't like admitting it, but you're right. Being isolated and sick has made me more selfish, making it easier for the enemy to slip in negative thoughts of despair. Yuck! What do I do?

I want you to stop thinking about yourself. I know the doctor said to rest and that's why you're watching more TV. However, you're not that sick, so I want you to get up and do something productive. Do you remember that your family suggested that you make masks for them?

Yeah, my children said that before, but I didn't want to. So, I guess I will now.

I'm pleased with your response. You're very creative and capable of making changes to make masks that are comfortable for your family. So, make some for your immediate family and your parents.

Okay, Lord. I'll start researching the various types of masks and make a version my family would like.

I'm pleased that you're going to get up and do something for someone else. Believe me, you will feel better.

...a few days later...

I'm embarrassed to admit it, Lord, but I started to feel a little better as I was sewing the masks. I'm not as negative or as selfish as before.

Thank you, Lord, for this *mini-trial*. I don't like it, but it's teaching me how selfishness allows the enemy to easily invade me with negative thoughts. This is a bit scary, so I need to be more aware of his tactics and arm myself with your Word. He's sneaky. He slowly turns one thought into an irritation that produces anger, creating more negativity and despair in me. He knows how to bring me down.

Yes, the enemy is sly and clever. He knows your weaknesses.

I know you forgive me for my selfishness. But I'm also embarrassed that because I'm sick, it brought out the worst in me. There are so many people in dire circumstances compared to me. So many people are suffering because of the pandemic, yet they have shown great courage and strength. So many have been generous to one another. I'm ashamed of my response. Lord, forgive me.

I will always forgive you. I know you're ashamed about how you reacted, but I'm glad you're aware of it. Some people don't want to face or admit their mistakes. But you allow me to show you your errors and help you learn from them.

You're also right that your incident is minor compared to the others that are suffering. The enemy is trying to bring everyone down and causing pain to many families. There are health problems, financial problems, and relationship problems. But when they come to me, I will heal their heart and soul. I will give them my peace that the world cannot give them.

Yes, heal their hearts, Lord. I pray that they feel your love and presence during this time. Please bring angels to their side. Hold their hands and give them rest and peace. Heal their hearts, Lord!

Heal me too, Lord! Stop me, so my selfishness doesn't overpower me.

As you seek me, you will pause for a moment and listen to me. Keep doing that, and I will always bring you out of your hole of despair and bring you upwards towards me! I love you. You are my precious child.

(At the time I'm writing this, I'm still battling my sickness. It's been about six months, but I see the light at the end of the tunnel.)

Reflections:

- How is the enemy, Satan, invading you with negative thoughts?
- What is God trying to tell you?

You Spit on the Man!

"They came to Bethsaida, and some people brought a blind man and begged Jesus to touch him. He took the blind man by the hand and led him outside the village. When he had spit on the man's eyes and put his hands on him, Jesus asked, 'Do you see anything?' He looked up and said, 'I see people; they look like trees walking around.' Once more, Jesus put his hands on the man's eyes. Then his eyes were opened, his sight was restored, and he saw everything clearly. Jesus sent him home, saying, 'Don't even go into the village'" (Mark 8:22-26, NIV).

Now reread this slowly, and let's talk.

You led the blind man outside the village. Why did you do that?

I gently took the blind man's hand and led him outside the village because I wanted to be alone with him. Just like that man, I want you to trust me as I guide you too. I want to be alone with you and away from your distractions. My time with that man was intimate and personal. That's what I want with you. I love it when you stop, sit beside me, and we discuss things.

Oh Lord, thank you for loving me and wanting to be with me. I understand that, but why did you spit on his eyes? That's so gross, Lord!

Sometimes you have to let me do something *yucky* in your life for me to help and heal you. You remember the *yucky stuff* more than the good things.

You're right, Lord. I hate to admit it, but I remember my trials or hard times more than daily blessings. So, if I want to grow in you, I have to let you do some *yucky stuff* in my life. I get it, Lord. I don't like it, but I understand it.

Just like that blind man, I want you to stop now, look up, and look straight at me with your eyes open.

Okay.

He couldn't see what I was about to do. But he trusted me to heal him! You need to have that same faith. You don't know what I'm about to do, but you need to trust *ME!* I know what I'm doing. I will heal you!

Yes, Lord. Why did you spit on his eyes and place your hands upon him twice?

I did it twice because I want my children to know that sometimes things take more time to be healed physically and spiritually. People always want or expect instant healing. But remember, my ways are not your ways. I know what's best for my children. My timing is perfect.

For you, sometimes, it takes you longer to let go of your control and let me handle the problem or situation. So, I have to let you experience *yucky stuff* again. It's necessary because it helps you give up that control. I do that because I love you so much.

Yes, it's hard for me to let go of my control. I know better, but it's so easy for me to slip in and take the reins of my life. Thank you for the second, third, and umpteen chances.

Then you sent the blind man home instead of going back to the village to tell everyone. Why? They would have believed in you because of the miracle you just performed.

Yes, I agree, but I don't want you or them to focus on the miracle. I want you to focus on *me!* By going home, he would be alone, thanking and praising God!

Yes, sitting with you, listening to you, and being with you always brings tears to my eyes. I will trust you to do some *yucky stuff* because you know what's best. I will also focus on you instead of taking the reins of my life.

Reflections:

- What *yucky stuff* is in your life now? What is God trying to show you?
- Is God prompting you to give up control in some area of your life?
- Do you need healing in your life right now? Are you willing to let God do something *yucky* to bring about that healing?

Wait and Listen, Then Do

"And he said to them, 'Truly I tell you, some who are standing here will not taste death before they see that the kingdom of God has come with power.' After six days, Jesus took Peter, James, and John with him and led them up a high mountain, where they were all alone. There he was transfigured before them. His clothes became dazzling white, whiter than anyone in the world could bleach them. And there appeared before them Elijah and Moses, who were talking with Jesus. Peter said to Jesus, 'Rabbi, it is good for us to be here. Let us put up three shelters—one for you, one for Moses and one for Elijah.' (He did not know what to say, they were so frightened.) Then a cloud appeared and covered them, and a voice came from the cloud: 'This is my Son, whom I love. Listen to him!' Suddenly, when they looked around, they no longer saw anyone with them except Jesus. As they were coming down the mountain, Jesus gave them orders not to tell anyone what they had seen until the Son of Man had risen from the dead. They kept the matter to themselves, discussing what 'rising from the dead' meant. And they asked him, 'Why do the teachers of the law say that Elijah must come first?' Jesus replied, 'To be sure, Elijah does come first, and restores all things. Why then is it written that the Son of Man must suffer much and be rejected? But I tell you, Elijah has come, and they have done to him everything they wished, just as it is written about him'" (Mark 9:1-13, NIV).

Lord, you took Peter, James, and John to a high mountain all alone. You like being alone, where it's quiet, and there are no distractions, huh?

Yes, I wanted to show them something important. It was just for Peter, James, and John. Sometimes I reveal things to certain people, not everyone. It's part of my plan. Now describe what you saw as you read those verses.

While everyone is up on the high mountain, you transform and reveal your true self to them.

I picture a bright light coming from you, so dazzling white that's it hard to look at you because you're so bright! Then I see Elijah and Moses talking with you! That's so cool!

Then Peter says something dumb. He says, *"Let's put up three shelters."* I guess he didn't know what to say because he was shocked and a bit scared. Why did he feel he needed to say or do something? Why didn't he just wait and watch?

I agree with you, but sometimes that's what you do.

Huh?

Peter is scared. He doesn't like that feeling. So, he needs to do or say something to help him deal with the fear he has. He's used to taking charge of things. So, he speaks instead of thinking. He was bold like you are. Instead, he should have waited and listened to me. Isn't that what I tell you too?

Yup. I've always identified with Peter. Sometimes he speaks and acts before he thinks.

So, don't be so hard on Peter.

Yeah. When I'm frustrated with myself, you've told me to be kind to myself and listen to you.

Yes, I want you to stop, wait, and listen to me. When you do that, then you're able to do what I say.

Yes, Lord. Thank you for making music too. It heals my soul. This incident reminds me of a song I love, "Wait on the Lord," by Randy

Thomas. I used to sing it a lot when I was younger. So, I'll start singing it again to guide me as we journey together.

Reflections:

- How are you like Peter?
- When and why is God telling you to stop, wait, and listen?
- What does God want you to do? Where to go? What to say?
- How is God trying to get you alone and away from your distractions to show you something?

Causes Me to Sin

"If anyone causes one of these little ones—those who believe in me—to stumble, it would be better for them if a large millstone were hung around their neck and they were thrown into the sea. If your hand causes you to stumble, cut it off. It is better for you to enter life maimed than with two hands to go into hell, where the fire never goes out. And if your foot causes you to stumble, cut it off. It is better for you to enter life crippled than to have two feet and be thrown into hell. And if your eye causes you to stumble, pluck it out. It is better for you to enter the kingdom of God with one eye than to have two eyes and be thrown into hell, where 'the worms that eat them do not die, and the fire is not quenched'" (Mark 9:42-48, NIV).

Eeww, Lord. Gross! I don't like those images of cutting your hand or foot off!

I know, but it gets the point across.

When the verses describe "Hell," it makes me shudder too. Like when the verses say, *"where the fire never goes out...and the worms eat them but do not die, and the fire is not quenched."* I remember that Christian man on TV describing his vision of visiting hell. You took him there so he could report back to us what he saw and felt. He said the description of hell is in the Bible, and they're all *true*! He felt them too! Eeww.

Yes, but don't get distracted here about the description of hell. What are these verses focusing on?

If I do something that causes a little one to stumble in their walk with you, I'm in big trouble! Teaching the little ones is a big responsibility.

They're at an age that is so impressionable. So, I better show your love to them through words and actions.

Yes, be an example to the little ones, but reread the verses to find the main focus. What causes you to stumble?

Hmmm...what causes me to stumble? Or is it more like, what causes me to sin? What do I do that makes you sad?

I'm saddened when you think about other people and put them down. You have these thoughts in your head, so nobody sees or hears them, but I do.

I understand. I'm so ashamed that you're right. When people hurt me or irritate me, I tend to compare myself to them and put them down silently in my head. I think, why are they doing that? Why are they so selfish or power-hungry? Why can't they do what is right? Why can't they focus on *you* instead of thinking about themselves? Oh my gosh, Lord! I'm so bad; forgive me for judging others.

I forgive you. I want you to see these people the way I *see* them. I know their weaknesses, but I also see their potential when they come to me. I love them, no matter what!

Yes, Lord. You see the good in me and my arrogance too, and you still love me no matter what. Help me focus on you when others say hurtful things to me, so I won't judge or put them down. I'm sorry, Lord. Please give me your eyes to see people the way you do.

Remember that phrase I gave you a while ago. "Trust and obey, no matter what people do and say."

Yes, Lord.

Reflections:

- What causes you to stumble, which leads to sin?
- Ask God to help you "cut" it out of your life.

Joseph of Arimathea

"It was Preparation Day (that is, the day before the Sabbath). So as evening approached, Joseph of Arimathea, a prominent member of the Council, who was himself waiting for the kingdom of God, went boldly to Pilate and asked for Jesus' body. Pilate was surprised to hear that he was already dead. Summoning the centurion, he asked him if Jesus had already died. When he learned from the centurion that it was so, he gave the body to Joseph. So Joseph bought some linen cloth, took down the body, wrapped it in the linen, and placed it in a tomb cut out of rock. Then he rolled a stone against the entrance of the tomb. Mary Magdalene and Mary, the mother of Joseph, saw where he was laid" (Mark 15:42-47, NIV).

I want you to look again at Joseph of Arimathea. Do you know who he is?

Yes, but I don't know that much about him. But according to verse 43, he was a prominent member of the Council. So, I assume he was in a high position and respected by others.

Yes, Joseph of Arimathea was a respected member of the Council. What did he do after Jesus died?

"...went boldly to Pilate & asked for Jesus' body..." He's bold! He needed the courage to go to Pilate. He might have been risking his reputation and high position. When he asked for Jesus' body, he revealed to everyone that he believed in Jesus. Verse 43 says, *"...himself waiting for the kingdom of God..."*

Yes, there were men in high positions that were honestly seeking the Messiah and open to Jesus. Do you remember the Pharisee, Nicodemus?

Yes, Nicodemus went to see Jesus privately and asked Him many questions. This gives me hope that people in high positions can have open hearts to you, Lord. Their knowledge and status won't blind them to the truth of knowing you, Lord.

Yes, they are precious servants of mine. Nicodemus was helping Joseph too. See John 19:39 (NIV), *"He was accompanied by Nicodemus, the man who earlier had visited Jesus at night. Nicodemus brought a mixture of myrrh and aloes, about seventy-five pounds."*

What did Joseph do next?

He bought linen cloth to wrap Jesus' body.

Joseph thought all of this through. He was organized and practical. He knew what he needed to do and get.

I like organized people. I never thought about him before until now.

What happened after Joseph bought the linen?

Pilate granted Joseph permission to get Jesus' body. So Joseph went to the cross. Yuck! That must have been a gruesome sight, Lord. I couldn't bear to see Jesus like that. That must have taken great strength of character on Joseph's part to see his beloved Jesus dripping in blood. Oh Lord, Joseph is amazing!

Yes, he was practical, organized, strong in character, and full of love for Jesus. I gave him those outstanding qualities to help him take care of Jesus' body.

Oh, Lord. I have so much respect for Joseph. I'm ashamed that I never read this passage slowly to understand the man who humbly took care of Jesus after he died.

I'm pleased that you slowed down to read it. What did Joseph do next?

Verse Mark 15:46 says, *"... took down the body..."*

Oh, man Lord! I didn't know he did that too! I picture his body limp and dripping with so much blood! It's too much to bear to see, let alone touch. Joseph had inner strength! He's beyond fantastic, Lord!

I know he is. What happened after that?

> Mark 15:46 continues, *"...wrapped <u>it</u> in the linen and placed <u>it</u> in a tomb cut out of rock. Then he rolled a stone against the entrance of the tomb"* (emphasis added).

The verse says "it" when referring to Jesus' body. This makes it sound like his body must have been grotesque that the body didn't look like a person anymore. Oh, man, Lord! I can't bear to think about it. But Joseph wrapped Jesus and then put his body in a tomb. Then he rolled a huge stone against the entrance too! He's strong and amazing!

Do you think that placing him in a tomb is a standard burial for people?

I'm not sure, but it sounds like a rich man's burial.

Yes, it is.

Why did you want Jesus to have a rich man's burial?

I had him placed in a tomb cut out of rock with a stone rolled against the entrance because I knew what would happen on the

third day. Since it was like a cave, people could walk inside and see the linens left without Jesus' body inside, instead of digging the ground to see if he was resurrected.

That's right! Your plans are always the best! You know what you're doing!

Yes. I also had Jesus' body in a tomb because it was the tradition to place a huge stone against the entrance. I wanted the opening to be securely shut because I knew people were skeptical about his resurrection. So, I wanted guards placed at the tomb.

> Matthew 27:62-66 (NIV) says, *"The next day, the one after Preparation Day, the chief priests and the Pharisees went to Pilate. 'Sir,' they said, 'we remember that while he was still alive, that deceiver said, "After three days I will rise again." So give the order for the tomb to be made secure until the third day. Otherwise, his disciples may come and steal the body and tell the people he raised from the dead. This last deception will be worse than the first.' 'Take a guard,' Pilate answered. 'Go, make the tomb as secure as you know how.' So they went and made the tomb secure by putting a seal on the stone and posting the guard."*

Your plans are precise, down to the last detail.

Yes, I made it hard for the disciples or anyone else to take Jesus' body away. This way, it would be difficult to explain the disappearance of his body. I knew what the skeptical people would say.

You're smart, Lord! You think of everything!

What happened next? Who else was there with Joseph?

Mary Magdalene and Mary, the mother of Joseph, were with him. Who are they?

I want you to look it up in a Bible dictionary or the Internet.

Okay, I'll look those things up.

So I searched on the internet, How did they bury people back then? It said,

"The typical tombs of Jesus' day involve a cave or excavation cut into a rocky cliff. Sometimes larger families or groups of families would use these burial areas together. There would be an outer chamber and an inner chamber. In the outer chamber, the body would be laid out on a type of bench or shelf, cut into the rock. After final farewells, a large round stone, usually rolled in a groove dug in the ground, would be moved into place to cover the tomb's entrance.

Poor people who could not afford a rock-hewn tomb, or foreigners who had no land, were buried in designated fields in vertical shafts. There is a reference to the Potter's Field purchase in the Gospels that describes these sorts of cemeteries for the poor and foreigners who died in Israel and needed a burial in Matthew 27:7."

https://hcscchurch.org/wp-content/uploads/2014/08/Death-and-Burial.pdf

I think if Joseph of Arimathea didn't take Jesus' body, he would have been buried with the poor people. I'm so thankful that Joseph of Arimathea obeyed you and was your vessel. It seems like a small thing, but it was essential. He sacrificed his reputation amongst his peers, humbled himself by taking his body down, wrapped him in linens, and provided the tomb. Joseph was such a noble and excellent man! I won't forget him. I have such respect and admiration for him now.

I'm pleased that you're learning more about Joseph of Arimathea. My servants may be humble or rich. Their financial status doesn't matter to me. I want them to be open and willing to obey me. So, I

have reasons when I place you in certain places and situations. Now, who is Mary, the mother of Joseph?

So I looked up...Who is Mary, the mother of Joseph? It sounds like Mary, the mother of Joseph, is Jesus' aunt or another Mary that followed him to meet his needs. Or she could have been the mother of one of the disciples.

http://www.livingwithfaith.org/blog/
who-was-the-other-mary-at-the-tomb

God, it really doesn't matter who Mary, the mother of Joseph, is. What matters is what she and Mary Magdalene did. I'm glad you put their names in the Bible because they took care of Jesus' needs in death and burial rituals. They were strong because that must have been a horrendous sight! I can't imagine or bear it. This shows genuine compassion and love. How wonderful and beautiful! You provided Jesus with tremendous support from these women, the emotional support of love and care. May I be like them and give support to others. I want my actions to speak louder than my words.

Yes, I am pleased with these humble and obedient servants. I want you to remember the organized, practical, and inner strength of Joseph of Arimathea. Don't forget the love and compassion from Mary Magdalene and Mary, the mother of Joseph.

Reflections:

- How can you be like Joseph of Arimathea or Mary, the mother of Joseph?
- Are you willing to risk your reputation as a follower of Jesus?
- What can you do today that shows others your love for Jesus?

Step In My Steps

My boss and managers weren't listening to the employees' concerns. We had spoken to them about our issues, but there wasn't any improvement. Ninety percent of the employees completed a survey to show the boss and managers that the concerns were not from a few individuals. The survey showed that most of the workers were upset with the company, and there were many concerns. In a meeting, we listened to the boss explain the plans for the following year. I was appalled that he didn't address any of the workers' concerns expressed in the survey. There was a short break, so I went to the bathroom to speak to God because I was frustrated and angry. God told me that I had to speak the truth for my fellow workers because I loved them. So, I told the truth with tears in my eyes. Afterward, the boss still didn't address our concerns. He just responded that he is the boss. The meeting just ended. Many workers rallied around me to support me and thanked me for what I did. Afterward, I talked to God.

Hey God,

This sucks! My job is full of crap now! I can't believe how the boss and managers are treating me! It is full of crap! I'm sorry for the language, but it's so bad! You told me to speak up for the sake of the others. Well, I did, and look what happened! The boss informed me that the managers are upset with me, so they won't be attending meetings when I am present. I can't believe how they're acting so unprofessionally and immaturely.

Yes, their actions are evident to the entire company. The boss emailed a letter to everyone, causing fear amongst the other workers. He wants them to know the consequences of speaking up. Their actions are drawing a definitive line between you and them. Everyone in the company sees that you are being mistreated.

Yes, Lord. I didn't want this to happen. After speaking the truth, I prayed that the boss and managers would reflect on what I said and the survey results. You told me not to add my comments to the survey but let other people voice their opinions and negative comments. If I included my thoughts, the boss and managers would rationalize that those comments came from me and brush them off. I wanted the boss to know that the majority of the workers had similar concerns and issues. When I told everyone at the meeting that I refrained from adding any comments, they were shocked. Later, many of them thanked me because it made their voices louder.

Now you understand why your obedience is crucial and how important it is to follow my specific instructions. Your obedience gave you strength and validity to what you said in that meeting.

I know you were praying for a positive response. However, trust me because I have a plan. In time, you'll see it forming. But for now, know that I'm pleased with your obedience. I know it was challenging for you to obey me. The days ahead will be more problematic. So, you need to stay close to me to get through all of this.

... a few days later ...

You're right, Lord; these days are unbearable! I can't believe what the management is saying about me. I feel like I'm walking in "garbage" every day and grumbling with tons of negative thoughts! I quietly cry when I'm alone at work and at home. Please help me!

I see your tears every day, and my heart aches for you too.

*(Now I see a vision of God before **me** as He's talking with me.)*

Look at me now, focus, and come with me. Do you see the path ahead?

Yup, I see lots of crap before me—literally, Lord! It looks like giant piles of cow dung!

I want you to take my hand and hold it. Now don't move or take a step. Please observe as I take a step into the pile of cow dung.

(He takes a step into the mess, raises his foot, and the footprint that is left in the mess is clean! But there's still a mess <u>around</u> the outside of his footprint!)

Now carefully put your foot in my footprint. Keep stepping in my footsteps that are clean.

(Step by step, as I walk in his footprints, I feel his presence and peace fill my entire body, my soul, and spirit!) Wow, Lord! This is amazing! I understand, Lord! When I turn to you, and we spend time together, that's when I'm *walking in your footsteps.* You're the only one that can give me peace and calmness that the world can't give me.

Yes, my child, you are slowly learning how much I love you. So, I will walk in the *mess for you.*

However, when the world distracts you, you stop walking in my footprints. You must constantly renew your mind every day and every minute. Keep your focus on me, then you'll be able to walk in my clean footprints.

Ah, yes, Lord! Thank you for taking some of this mess so I can walk forward.

Some of the mess is still there, but it won't affect you when you walk carefully in my footprints. I see the unjust treatment that's being thrown at you. You're suffering because you told the truth. I'm proud of you! So let's keep walking together. I'll protect you, but you have to keep abiding and focusing on me.

Yes, Lord. I wish you would take away all of this mess, but if you did, I wouldn't walk carefully in your footprints and seek you daily.

Yes, my precious child.

The journey was long, but together we finished the path that was ahead. Thank you, God, for walking ahead of me and protecting me. People at my job told me, "As the dirt is being flung at you, you look whiter than snow. Being a Christian makes you different from them." When I heard encouraging words like that, tears flooded my heart. I was so touched by their support! They thanked me for speaking the truth. You knew I needed to hear encouraging remarks from multitudes of people. Thank you, Lord, for helping me shine your light and be your vessel. Several months later, most of those people who were disrespectful toward me were told to leave. Thank you, Lord!

> *"And God is able to bless you abundantly, so that in all things at all times, having all that you need, you will abound in every good work"* (2 Corinthians 9:8, NIV).

> *"And God is able to make all grace [every favor and earthly blessing] come in abundance to you, so that you may always [under all circumstances, regardless of the need] have complete sufficiency in everything [being completely self-sufficient in Him], and have an abundance for every good work and act of charity"* (2 Corinthians 9:8, AMP).

Reflections:

- What "crap" are you experiencing in life?
- How are you leaning on and waiting on the Lord for HIS guidance during this trial of your life?
- Are you walking in his footsteps?

Searching

"Every year, Jesus' parents went to Jerusalem for the Festival of the Passover. When he was twelve years old, they went up to the festival, according to the custom. After the festival was over, while his parents were returning home, the boy Jesus stayed behind in Jerusalem, but they were unaware of it. Thinking he was in their company, they traveled on for a day. Then they began looking for him among their relatives and friends. When they did not find him, they went back to Jerusalem to look for him. After three days, they found him in the temple courts, sitting among the teachers, listening to them and asking them questions. Everyone who heard him was amazed at his understanding and his answers. When his parents saw him, they were astonished. His mother said to him, 'Son, why have you treated us like this? Your father and I have been anxiously searching for you.'

'Why were you searching for me?' he asked. 'Didn't you know I had to be in my Father's house?' But they did not understand what he was saying to them.

Then he went down to Nazareth with them and was obedient to them. But his mother treasured all these things in her heart" (Luke 2:41-51, NIV).

I remember this story, Lord. Mary and Joseph must have been frantic looking for their son, Jesus! I would if I couldn't find my child!

I want you to reread the part about how long they were searching for Jesus.

"After three days, they found him in the temple courts..."

They were searching for three days! Three days is too long, Lord! As the days were going by, their stress and worrying must have been overwhelming! Mary must have been frantic because *you* entrusted *your son* to *her*! If she lost him, that would have been unbearable!

Yes, I understand all the stress and worry that was occurring. But all that anxiety could have been avoided.

Huh? How?

I want you to reread where they found him.

Lord it says, *"...they found Him in the temple courts..."*

Where is he?

Jesus is in the temple courts, which is God's house.

Now look again at Jesus' response to his mother.

> *"'Why were you searching for me?' he asked. 'Didn't you know I had to be in my Father's house?'"*

Hmmm. Jesus' question to his mom is logical. Why didn't they go to the temple first? They should have gone there, not necessarily to search for him, but to pray for wisdom. If they did, they would have seen him.

Now, let's not be self-righteous. You're just like the parents. What do you do when things don't go your way?

Forgive me, Lord. You're right. When things don't go my way, I get upset. I start worrying too. I take matters into my own hands and try to solve the problem or situation.

Yes, you do. Instead of worrying, why don't you come to me first? If you did, I would tell you, "Stop your negative thinking. Don't think

about how to solve the problem. Instead, I want you to come and sit quietly before me. I want you to bow down and then look up at *me!*"

I would stretch out my hands, cup your face in my palms and say, "Why are you worrying? You don't need to panic or get upset. I'm always here for you. Remember, everything is under control. I know how you're feeling. I want you to relax and remember that my plan is the best. I know what I'm doing."

What's your favorite verse?

My favorite verse is *"Trust in the Lord, your God with all your heart and lean not onto thy own understanding. In all thy ways, acknowledge Him, and He shall direct thy paths"* (Proverbs 3:5-6, KJV).

I'm sorry, Lord, that I'm not trusting you with all my heart. Please help me to trust you, Lord, no matter what happens. I don't want to rely on myself and what I think I can do. Please guide me in *your way, Lord,* and instruct me as to what I should do.

Thank you, Lord, for being patient with me when I take matters into my own hands and try to control things I really can't control. I'm sorry that you have to wait for me to come to you.

I love you, so I will always wait for you. I just want you to come sooner so I can lessen your anxiety.

Reflections:

- What are you worrying about?
- What matters are you taking into your own hands?
- Who do you turn to during your time of need—self, man, or God?

Don't Be Busy; Sit by Me

"While Jesus was in one of the towns, a man came along who was covered with leprosy. When he saw Jesus, he fell with his face to the ground and begged him, 'Lord, if you are willing, you can make me clean.' Jesus reached out his hand and touched the man. 'I am willing,' he said. 'Be clean!' And immediately, the leprosy left him. Then Jesus ordered him, 'Don't tell anyone, but go, show yourself to the priest and offer the sacrifices that Moses commanded for your cleansing, as a testimony to them.' Yet the news about him spread all the more so that crowds of people came to hear him and to be healed of their sicknesses. But Jesus often withdrew to lonely places and prayed" (Luke 5:12-16, NIV).

Jesus heals the man with leprosy. The man says, *"if you are willing."* This shows the man has faith and believes in Jesus.

Yes, but I want you to focus on what Jesus said to the man *after* he heals him.

Verse 14 says, *"Then Jesus ordered him..."* Wow, I don't remember hearing Jesus giving orders. I forget he wasn't a quiet man. I've always heard the world portray Him as mild and meek. He was kind and loving but also strong! Okay, so since Jesus ordered the man, what he says next must be important.

Yes, it is crucial, so continue reading.

Jesus orders him, *"Don't tell anyone, but go, show yourself to the priest and offer the sacrifices that Moses commanded for your cleansing, as a testimony to them"* (Luke 5:14).

When I was younger, I never understood why Jesus didn't want people to know he was the Son of God! Then as I grew older, I understood. If people knew he was the Son of God, then they wouldn't have crucified Jesus. He wouldn't have been able to fulfill your plan of salvation.

I have a plan, and I know what's best for you. Since you're learning that more, you're trusting me more and more. I'm pleased you're maturing in your faith. You're starting to say, "Not my will, but your will, Lord."

I also wanted the man to focus on gratitude to God instead of being a spectacle for everyone to see. People focused on Jesus' miracles instead of focusing on what he was telling them.

I want you to come to me with a humble, grateful, and thankful heart. I want a relationship with you. I want to talk with you. Unfortunately, some Christians are too busy doing things for me that they forget to meet with me. There's nothing wrong with doing things that please me that bring me glory. I appreciate their work, but I really just want to sit and talk and refresh their hearts.

Oh, yes, Lord! I love it when I feel your gentle breeze blowing and the leaves softly rustle when I sit outside. It's like you're whispering to me. Awww, your soft and gentle touch.

I don't want you doing too many things for me. I can do anything. I don't need your help. I can touch souls without your hard work of creating programs, etc. Just keep seeking me instead of making programs. My people need to rest in me more.

Yup, you're teaching me to rest more for physical and spiritual strength. Is that why the next verse says, *"But Jesus often withdrew to lonely places and prayed."* He needed to get refreshed by you, Lord, huh?

Yes, Jesus needed strength from me, physical rest, and "being with me." You do too!

Okay, Lord, I will sit before you, be quiet, gain strength, and be by you! You touch and refresh my soul!

Reflections:

- Take a moment to stop and sit quietly with the Lord.
- Are you too busy working for Jesus that it's hard to take time to sit in his presence?
- Make a concentrated effort to set time aside with him each day.

Pull Out the Weeds

While a large crowd was gathering and people were coming to Jesus from town after town, he told this parable: "A farmer went out to sow his seed. As he was scattering the seed, some fell along the path; it was trampled on, and the birds ate it up. Some fell on rocky ground, and when it came up, the plants withered because they had no moisture. Other seed fell among thorns, which grew up with it and choked the plants. Still other seed fell on good soil. It came up and yielded a crop, a hundred times more than was sown." When he said this, he called out, "Whoever has ears to hear, let them hear." His disciples asked him what this parable meant. He said, "The knowledge of the secrets of the kingdom of God has been given to you, but to others, I speak in parables, so that "though seeing, they may not see; though hearing, they may not understand.'

"This is the meaning of the parable: The seed is the word of God. Those along the path are the ones who hear, and then the devil comes and takes away the word from their hearts, so that they may not believe and be saved. Those on the rocky ground are the ones who receive the word with joy when they hear it, but they have no root. They believe for a while, but in the time of testing, they fall away. The seed that fell among thorns stands for those who hear, but as they go on their way, they are choked by life's worries, riches, and pleasures, and they do not mature. But the seed on good soil stands for those with a noble and good heart, who hear the word, retain it, and by persevering produce a crop." (Luke 8:4-15, NIV)

I've read and heard this parable many times. So, show me something new, Lord.

Okay, reread verses 6 and 7, then 13 and 14.

Verses 6 and 7: "Some fell on rocky ground, and when it came up, the plants withered because they had no moisture. Other seed fell among thorns, which grew up with it and choked the plants."

Verses 13 and 14: "Those on the rocky ground are the ones who receive the word with joy when they hear it, but they have no root They believe for a while, but in the time of testing, they fall away. So the seed that fell among thorns stands for those who hear, but as they go on their way, they are choked by life's worries, riches, and pleasures, and they do not mature."

I need you to help those people on the rocky ground and among the thorns. The seeds that fell on the rocky ground need more soil. So, you can *add soil* to the rocks and help the seeds grow.

How?

You add soil by being that person who comes alongside them. You can give them your support, your friendship, your love, and your listening ear.

I see, Lord. What about the seeds that fell among the thorns?

Together, we will *dig out* those *thorns and the weeds* amongst the plants. They represent barriers to me. Some people put up walls to protect themselves. They convince themselves they're right, get distracted by the world and its pleasures, so these people can't see that they need me.

How do I break those walls or barriers?

It's the same as adding the soil. You love the people instead of judging them. You give them your friendship, your support, and your listening ear. Then I will help them pull out those thorns and weeds. You need to be there for them as they go through this difficult time.

Wow, Lord. I never saw this before. I thought those seeds or people were lost. I never thought that I could help them. Thank you for showing me that I can help. Your wisdom and love always amaze me!

Don't accept the fact that some people are too stubborn or hurt to come to me. So many of my followers give up on them, but I don't want you to. I gave you that "stubbornness or perseverance" trait. So, keep adding soil and pulling out the thorns and weeds by being a true friend. One day those plants will get sunlight. They will flourish with me as they finally see the sun, my Son, Jesus!

Reflections:

- Who needs some soil added to their rocky ground?
- Who needs some weeding?
- Think of a simple way to start being a true friend and show that person you care.
- Do you need more soil or weeds to be pulled out?

Dig and Fertilize

"Then he told this parable: 'A man had a fig tree growing in his vineyard, and he went to look for fruit on it but did not find any. So he said to the man who took care of the vineyard, "For three years now I've been coming to look for fruit on this fig tree and haven't found any. Cut it down! Why should it use up the soil?" "Sir," the man replied, "leave it alone for one more year, and I'll dig around it and fertilize it. If it bears fruit next year, fine! If not, then cut it down"'" Luke 13:6-9 (NIV).

We are those fig trees that aren't producing, huh, Lord?

Yes, you are, but you can also be that man that says I'll dig around it and fertilize it.

I understand fertilizing, but why dig around the fig tree?

Digging around the tree will create a barrier. Help the people dig their trench by reading the Bible and spending time with me. It will help contain the fertilizer, so the tree will benefit from all of the fertilizer and, therefore, all of the nutrients it needs. I want you to start digging this trench to support your fellow brothers and sisters in Christ. Support them by calling them up, listening, and encouraging them in their Christian walk with me. I don't want you to complete the trench because people need to learn how to dig the trench for themselves. They will see what you're doing and learn from you.

I understand. It's like that old saying about, "Don't give someone a fish, but teach him to fish."

As they spend time in the Bible and time with me, my words and promises will be in their hearts, protect them from worldly distractions, and strengthen their faith.

Now let's look at the fertilizing part. Fertilizer doesn't smell good. It stinks! Sometimes growth hurts or stinks! But I know the plans I have for that person. I know what's needed, and my timing is the best. Of course, there are times when you want to jump in and give direction or advice, but remember, my ways are not your ways. So, you must *let me add* the fertilizer, not you. However, there will be times when I'll tell you to add it for me.

Yes, Lord. I continuously need you by my side as I dig trenches and you provide fertilizer for my friends. I need to be there for them as the fertilizer comes. Your specific words never cease to amaze me!

Reflections:

- Do you see a need to "dig a trench" in your life or a fellow brother or sister in Christ?
- Who can help teach you how to "dig a trench" and strengthen your faith?
- Are you adding the fertilizer instead of waiting for God to do it?
- Who does God want you to come alongside since the fertilizer is there?

The Mustard Seed

"Then Jesus asked, 'What is the kingdom of God like? What shall I compare it to? It is like a mustard seed, which a man took and planted in his garden. It grew and became a tree, and the birds perched in its branches'" (Luke 13:18-21, NIV).

The mustard seed is tiny. It appears to be insignificant, but look at how big it GROWS! I want you to write the stages you read in that passage. Then I'll show you what they mean.

Okay......

    1.   The man took the mustard seed.

When you were younger, you didn't know that there were two steps to becoming a Christian. The first step is believing that I died on the cross for you and rose again three days later. The next step is to pray and ask me to forgive you of your sins. When you do that, it is a humbling experience. Then as you pray to me for guidance in your life, I will bless you abundantly.

Yeah, I remember when I was young, I didn't know I had to pray and ask you to forgive my sins. People asked me if I believed in you. I said yes, but I didn't confess my sins and ask you to come into my life. I understand that believing is one thing, but giving my life to you is different.

Yes, when you ask me to forgive your sins, you are accepting my gift of salvation. This is called repenting. As you ask me to guide you, you learn to trust and obey me. Remember, I told you that Satan believes in me as other people do, but he won't bow down to me. Many people think that believing in me is enough to get them

into heaven, but it isn't. They have to humble themselves before me, repent, and follow me.

So, the first thing to do is to pray to accept Jesus Christ as my Savior. He is my Savior because he saved me from going to hell when he died on the cross and rose from the dead. When I ask for forgiveness, Jesus comes into my heart and life. Then when you see me, you see Jesus in me, so I can enter into heaven. Thank you for saving me and being my Savior!

Yes. However, some people think it's too easy to say the "sinner's prayer" to get into heaven. But saying this prayer is a hard thing to do because you have to mean it. I see everyone's inner thoughts and hearts. I know when they're telling the truth. It's hard for people to trust and obey me because everyone wants to control their lives instead of following me.

Yes, Lord. I know many people like that. My heart cries as I pray for them.

2. The seed is planted.

That's when you prayed to accept Jesus Christ as your Savior. Do you remember the day I came into your life?

I wish I had written the date down, but I remember where I was. I was in the church's youth group room, and I was sitting on a couch. As I reflect on that day, tears are flowing because that's when you touched my soul! Thank you, Lord!

3. Then, the seed grows.

This is the most essential part. For a seed to grow, it needs good soil, sunshine, and water. If a seed doesn't get *one* of those things, it won't grow. Likewise, just having water won't help it grow. Remember when you drowned the cactus by overwatering it?

Yup. The cactus died.

Like the plant, you need good soil, sunshine, and water. You need these too. The *"good soil"* is your open heart to hear what I'm saying. The *"sunshine"* is you reading my Word, the Bible. The *"water"* is when you learn and apply what I say. Sometimes people read and gain knowledge, but they don't use it in their life. So be aware of that.

When all the components are present and working, only then will a seed sprout. Just like a plant that grows, our relationship keeps growing as you get to know me more and more. Having this relationship with you is the most important thing to me! I love talking with you and being by your side in joyous times and hard times.

I love that too, Lord! I don't know what I would do without you. Thank you for loving me so much that you call me your daughter and love spending time with me. I'm so grateful for your love!

I love you; you're my precious daughter! So, what's the next step or stage?

4. The seed grows into a tree.

As the little plant grows, it gets more prominent as it draws strength from the good soil, sunshine, and water. It grows into a strong tree with roots that go down deep into the ground. As you keep reading my Word, listening to me, trusting, and obeying me, you become more mature. You become a deep, rooted tree that won't be swayed when tough times come into your life. You have a strong, solid foundation in me.

Yes, but trusting and obeying you is the hard part for me.

I remember you telling me something similar to what Pastor Wayne Cordeiro said,

As I read more,
I get to know you more
and so, I trust you more.
When I trust you more,
it's easier to obey you more.

Exactly! That's why I want you to keep reading and talking with me. Now, what's the last step?

5.   Finally, the tree becomes a home for the birds.

The tree doesn't stop growing. As it flourishes, it provides a home for the birds. So you should give support and love to your brothers and sisters in Christ and others who don't know me. The tree grows big and looks inviting to the birds. As you grow in me, then your life will be appealing to others. So be my vessel of love and provide a shelter of support for others.

Summary:

First, you get the mustard seed	*Hear about accepting Christ.
Then you plant it into the ground	*Pray and confess your sins to Christ and give your life to Him
Next, the seed grows	*Have an open heart, read the Bible, apply
Then it becomes a tree	*Build a strong, firm foundation and relationship with Christ
Finally, that tiny mustard seed becomes a home for the birds	*Provide love and support to others.

Invite others to Christ!

Thank you, Lord, for discussing each stage of the mustard seed's growth and how it applies to my life. Help me to continue to grow in you.

(Then I went outside to take my dogs out and see God's creation. I had a yearning to see my unique tree. It has two huge branches that form a "V" shape. The branches look like my two arms, opening and stretching up towards God. God continued our conversation.)

Lord, as I sit here outside by my tree in the backyard, I gaze upon your creations that surround me. I'm relaxed when I'm amongst your creation...the grass, the leaves, the birds, the flowers, and your gentle breeze. They bring me peace and calmness.

Yes, everything I create has a purpose. The nature that surrounds you was created for you. If that's true, doesn't it make sense that I created you with a specific purpose too?

Yes, you've been telling me this for a while. You created me for a specific purpose. When I surrender to you, I will fulfill my purpose and use the potential you have given me. You created me with specific traits, like my stubbornness or perseverance and sassy attitude. However, these traits have helped me survive many trials. I used to view them as my weaknesses, but I'm beginning to see that they are my strengths as I rely on you, Lord! It's amazing how you turn my negative thoughts about myself and use them for positive outcomes. Like the verse says...

> *"But he said to me, 'My grace is sufficient for you, for my power is made perfect in weakness.' Therefore I will boast all the more gladly about my weaknesses so that Christ's power may rest on me. That is why, for Christ's sake, I delight in weaknesses, in insults, in hardships, in persecutions, in difficulties. For when I am weak, then I am strong'"* (2 Corinthians 12:9-11, NIV).

The sassy attitude and perseverance you gave me helped me stand firm and not give up the fight against injustice at work. It also gave me strength as I attended a hearing to discuss many co-workers' unfair treatment. An advisor told me he was impressed at how I handled the mediator. I told him I didn't want to answer any questions because I saw how they twisted my co-worker's answers and made her look guilty. My sassy attitude or boldness kicked in when I explained to the mediator that his job was to learn about the truth and not be confused with the other side's questions. So, I asked for permission to not answer questions but to tell him my story of what happened at work. He permitted me to do that. My boldness helped the rest of my co-workers, who would testify, to follow my example. As each one went up, my co-workers didn't answer questions. Instead, they told their story.

Yes, I remember that day, and your group won! Of course, you were very anxious, but your co-workers looked to you and another worker as leaders. I was so pleased that they asked you to pray for guidance and wisdom.

That's right, Lord! You gave me wisdom that day! Thank you!

Now you're learning how everything I create has a purpose. So, you're right about your weaknesses. But, I've never seen them as weaknesses because I have always known they are your strengths! The mustard seed illustration shows you the Christian journey, but steps four and five are where many Christians pause as the world distracts them. So, keep your focus on me, and continue meeting with me. I will guide you as you journey with me.

Yes, Lord, help me to focus on you! Thank you, Lord, for the reminder that I was created with a specific purpose to fulfill, and you don't make mistakes when you create your children. You know what you're doing.

Reflections:

- How are you growing in your journey with God? Where would you say you are in the process, when you compare it to the mustard seed?
- Has God shown you how He has used one of your weaknesses as a strength? Ask Him to show you.
- Do you want to accept Jesus Christ as your Savior? Look at "Start Your Spark."

Lightening My Hair

(I started to bleach my facial hair above my upper lip. Then, I made the mixture and placed it on. The directions say to keep the paste mixture on for about fifteen minutes or so. I was about to set the timer on my phone, but God stopped me.)

Stop! I don't want you to set a timer. I want you to rinse it off when it's done.

Huh? How will I know when it's done?

You'll know when it's ready to rinse everything off because one part will fall off by itself.

This is strange, but okay, I won't set a timer. You're funny, Lord.

(After applying the mixture, I went to do some work. I don't know how much time passed, but some of it fell off.)

Now it's time to go and rinse it all off.

Okay, but let me finish this task. I'm almost done.

(Then I go to the bathroom and start to rinse the bleach off. I usually have to rinse it multiple times because there's usually some mixture that doesn't come off quickly. However, this time, everything just fell off really fast! I was shocked!)

Wow, that was fast, God! So now I can get back to what I was doing. Thanks, God!

No, I don't want you to go back to what you were doing. There's a lesson I want you to learn. Why was it faster to rinse the mixture off of you this time compared to the other times?

I guess it was faster because I left it on without disturbing it or rushing it. Usually, I check to see if the bleach mixture is done because I don't like waiting.

Yes, you usually stop and check the mixture because you're impatient and don't like waiting.

Yup! That's me!

But this time, you were doing something else. So, you didn't check it and test to see if it was ready to rinse. You didn't meddle. Do you understand my lesson?

I don't have to set a timer; just wait! No, I'm kidding God!

I think I understand your lesson! You don't want me to meddle and rush things.

Yes, I don't want you to solve the problem or situation because I have everything under control. I have a plan. Instead, I want you to focus on me and obey me. Then your mind won't be consumed with the problem or situation. Instead, you will be focused on a task I'm giving you. Remember, my ways are not your ways.

The bleach mixture fell off fast, right?

Yeah, I liked that it was quick! It was faster to clean my face!

That's the way it is with the situation you're facing now. When it's *my time*, everything will be fast! So be prepared; it will be quick and impressive! Everything will fall into place because it's my plan!

Wow! You have a sense of humor, God! I love it when you use everyday situations to teach me something. I remember this more because it's kind of silly. Thank you for stopping me and teaching me this important lesson of not meddling. You want me to trust you because you have a plan, a perfect plan!

I'm glad you recognized my voice and stopped!

Reflections:

- What are you trying to solve on your own instead of asking God for help?
- What task does God want you to focus on instead of focusing on the problem or situation?

The Lost Coin

"Or suppose a woman has ten silver coins and loses one. Doesn't she light a lamp, sweep the house and search carefully until she finds it? And when she finds it, she calls her friends and neighbors together and says, 'Rejoice with me; I have found my lost coin.' In the same way, I tell you, there is rejoicing in the presence of the angels of God over one sinner who repents" (Luke 15:8-10, NIV).

Usually, this passage refers to me as the woman, and the coins are people. The lost coin is the lost soul or sinner. Then when that sinner repents, the angels of God rejoice!

But they also rejoice when the believer surrenders to me and puts me first in their life.

Let's take another look at the woman and the coin to help you answer your friend's question. She asked you, "How can I have two-way conversations with God? I want a close relationship with him."

You are the woman, and the coin you are searching for is "having a close relationship with me." So first, let's examine how the woman searches for her coin. Then I want you to share it with your friend.

Now reread this and then write down the things she does to find her lost coin.

She lights a lamp.

The lamp represents the Bible. It's your light or guide for your life.

She sweeps the house.

Sweeping represents when I cleanse you of your hurts, your frustration, and your doubts. After sweeping you, you're free and open to listen to me.

She searches carefully and then finds the coin.

I want you to be like that woman. She was searching and *doing something* instead of just sitting and waiting. She didn't expect the coin to appear miraculously. She did her part. You are searching carefully when you read my Word and listen to what I tell you. When you start putting me first in your life, you'll begin trusting and obeying me more. Then you'll find the *coin* or have a close relationship with me.

These are simple directions, but it's hard to follow. Sometimes it's a struggle because I want *my way* instead of surrendering to you or putting you first in my life.

I know it's hard to let go of the reins of your life. The world teaches you to be independent and take charge of your life and destiny. However, as you read my Word more, listen to me more, trust me, and obey me more, you will be able to let go of the reins of your life a little more every day. What Word am I repeating?

You're repeating the Word, *"More."* I understand; the *more* I read, listen, trust, and obey you, I will get closer to you and be able to let go of my life *more*. When I do, you and the angels rejoice!

Yes, we rejoice when the lost sinner repents and when the believer starts surrendering their life and starts following me. It's the beginning of having a close relationship with me!

Nothing replaces reading your Word and putting you first in my life. When I do, I will find the coin or the peace of God in my heart and have a close relationship with you!

Yes, so now go and tell your friend; our two-way conversations didn't just happen overnight. It started when you first sat down to read the Bible, and you listened to me. Then over time, you slowly surrendered parts of your life to me and started obeying me more than before.

Okay, I will share this with my friend. But I know in the beginning, it's hard to set aside time for you, Lord. So, when I became a new Christian, I asked you, "How will I find extra time?"

You said, wake up fifteen minutes earlier and read the Bible or devotion each day. Pray anywhere with your eyes open. For example, pray when you're driving to work.

Yes, I did. The important thing is to start reading my Word and sitting with me.

Reflections:

- Do you want to have two-way conversations with the Lord?
- Is reading the Word of God a priority for you?
- God knows and sees your life. Ask Him how to make some minor changes so you can meet with Him more.

Watching and Waiting

Jesus continued: *"There was a man who had two sons. The younger one said to his father, 'Father, give me my share of the estate.' So he divided his property between them.* *"Not long after that, the younger son got together all he had, set off for a distant country and there squandered his wealth in wild living. After he had spent everything, there was a severe famine in that whole country, and he began to be in need. So he went and hired himself out to a citizen of that country, who sent him to his fields to feed pigs. He longed to fill his stomach with the pods that the pigs were eating, but no one gave him anything.*

"When he came to his senses, he said, 'How many of my father's hired servants have food to spare, and here I am starving to death! I will set out and go back to my father and say to him: Father, I have sinned against heaven and against you. I am no longer worthy to be called your son; make me like one of your hired servants.' So, he got up and went to his father.

"But while he was still a long way off, his father saw him and was filled with compassion for him; he ran to his son, threw his arms around him and kissed him. The son said to him, 'Father, I have sinned against heaven and against you. I am no longer worthy to be called your son.' But the Father said to his servants, 'Quick! Bring the best robe and put it on him. Put a ring on his finger and sandals on his feet. Bring the fattened calf and kill it. Let's have a feast and celebrate. For this son of mine was dead and is alive again; he was lost and is found.' So, they began to celebrate.

"Meanwhile, the older son was in the field. When he came near the house, he heard music and dancing. So, he called one of the servants and asked him what was going on. 'Your brother has come,'

he replied, 'and your father has killed the fattened calf because he has him back safe and sound.' The older brother became angry and refused to go in. So, his father went out and pleaded with him. But he answered his father, 'Look! All these years I've been slaving for you and never disobeyed your orders. Yet you never gave me even a young goat so I could celebrate with my friends. But when this son of yours who has squandered your property with prostitutes comes home, you kill the fattened calf for him!'

"'My son,' the father said, 'you are always with me, and everything I have is yours." (Luke 15:11-31, NIV)

You know this story about the Prodigal Son. You've heard it many times. But I want you to reread verse 20 slowly.

Okay. *"So he got up and went to his father. But while he was still a long way off, his father saw him."*

STOP there!

Did the dad just go outside at that particular time to look for him? How would he know what day to go out and look?

I don't think going outside at that specific time was by chance.

Yes, it would be highly improbable. Every day, his dad would go outside waiting and watching for his son to return.

That's just like you, Lord. You're always waiting and watching for us to come to you. Your patience is incredible! God, you understand the feeling of *waiting*.

The son didn't know or feel that his dad was waiting and watching for him.

I understand the son because I forget you're waiting and watching me too. Sometimes I don't feel it either, but you are always there for me, whether I feel it or not.

Yes. The father wasn't watching from inside. He didn't look out the window occasionally; he intentionally went out every day and waited and watched!

This is what you do for me every day too. You're always watching over me. You see everything I'm doing and feeling. You see and feel my tears. That's when you wait and watch for me to come to you. You don't force me; you wait lovingly and patiently.

Yes, I do wait for you. But the father didn't wait for his son to be at his feet. So what did he do instead?

He ran toward his son!

Listen carefully. You think I'm far away from you, a long-distance out. You think I want you to come to me and work hard to get to me by reading the Bible and being good. I don't need you to walk a long way to reach me and be at my feet. I just want you to look up and face me wherever you are at that moment. I will see your attitude of repentance. Then, I will run toward you! I know you're hurting, and it's so hard to come to me. I understand, so I'll run to you and then carry you!

Yes! A long time ago, you did that for me. I told you I wanted to come to you, but I was so weak and hurt. I felt like I couldn't even walk to you. I remember telling you, "I know you want me to come of my own free will, but I can't move forward. I don't know what to do. Please push or pull me towards you! I need you now!"

Yes, I remember that day too. That's when I told you, "You don't have to walk a long way to come to me. I will run to you. I'm right

beside you now. I just want you to come to me as you are." So, then I picked you up and carried you.

Yes, that's when I truly surrendered my life to you. I prayed to accept you as my Savior before, but I only opened up a part of my life. But that day, I gave you all of me!

Thank you, Lord, for always watching and waiting for me and running towards me as the father ran to his son.

Reflections:

- When do you feel weak and stuck in where you are?
- Have you ever thought about God watching and waiting for you to come to him?
- Can you imagine him running towards you? How does that make you feel?
- How has God welcomed you back into his fold after you walked away from him?

What's Your Excuse?

"There was a rich man who was dressed in purple and fine linen and lived in luxury every day. At his gate was laid a beggar named Lazarus, covered with sores and longing to eat what fell from the rich man's table. Even the dogs came and licked his sores. The time came when the beggar died, and the angels carried him to Abraham's side. The rich man also died and was buried. In Hades, where he was in torment, he looked up and saw Abraham far away, with Lazarus by his side. So he called to him, 'Father Abraham, have pity on me and send Lazarus to dip the tip of his finger in water and cool my tongue because I am in agony in this fire.'

"But Abraham replied, 'Son, remember that in your lifetime you received your good things, while Lazarus received bad things, but now he is comforted here, and you are in agony. And besides all this, between us and you a great chasm has been set in place so that those who want to go from here to you cannot, nor can anyone cross over from there to us.'

"He answered, 'Then I beg you, father, send Lazarus to my family, for I have five brothers. Let him warn them so that they will not also come to this place of torment.'

"Abraham replied, 'They have Moses and the Prophets; let them listen to them.' 'No, father Abraham,' he said, 'but if someone from the dead goes to them, they will repent.'

"He said to him, 'If they do not listen to Moses and the Prophets, they will not be convinced even if someone rises from the dead.'"
(Luke 16:19-31, NIV).

What stands out to you?

The rich man knew the beggar because he called him by the name "Lazarus."

Yes, Lazarus wasn't just a beggar, but someone this rich man knew. He saw him all the time outside by his gate.

Wow, Lord. He saw him, knew him, and he still didn't help him. That's sad and rather self-righteous of that rich man. He could've spared some leftovers.

You're like that rich man too. I put people in your life because I want you to help them. It's not a coincidence that you meet certain people and get to know them. I placed them there, so please help them.

Yes, Lord. Help me be your servant. I'm embarrassed, but my selfishness prevents me from helping others and obeying you. I remember thinking, "I'm too tired to call that person now," or "I'm too busy to help. I want to do something for myself instead." I've questioned you about giving money to others since I don't have much. I'm so selfish, Lord. Help me.

Remember what I told you in a vision while in high school about giving excuses?

Oh, yes, Lord! I was with you, and we were standing by the gate to heaven. I hugged you, and I was so happy! Then I heard someone yell my name! I looked around and didn't see anyone. Then the voice cried, "Look down over here!" I looked down and saw hell with blazing flames of fire! The voice yelled, "Why didn't you tell me about God?" I looked at you, Lord, with tears in my eyes.

Yes, I saw your tears and asked you, "What are you going to say to that person? There isn't any excuse that's good enough. You can't

say you were too busy, tired, scared, or don't know enough about God. Those aren't good reasons or excuses. There's nothing you can say but that you're sorry for being selfish. So, *remember* what I'm telling you. Now *go* back to Earth, spread my word, and tell people about my love!"

Yes, I remember Lord, even though it happened so long ago. It shook me up and scared me! I don't ever want a friend of mine to say those words, "Why didn't you tell me about God?" Thank you for reminding me of that vision.

Reflections:

- What person in your life needs to hear about God's Love?
- What excuse(s) are you giving God for why you can't share?

Mother's Day

Hey God,

The world's expectations screw me up, huh, Lord? I didn't say anything to my family, but I was hurt on Mother's Day. My children didn't give me anything or say anything. They forgot it was Mother's Day. My husband remembered it was Mother's Day, so he was upset with them. He told them that they're grown adults and are responsible for taking care of their mom instead of him. I agreed with him, but I was still hurt.

Yes, I know you were hurt. I saw and felt your tears.

The world tells us that on Mother's Day, we're to be showered with beautiful gifts and praise! We're to be treated like a queen because mothers are fantastic! So, the children should do amazing things for their mom on this day! That's what we hear in the commercials!

Yes, the world has turned Mother's Day into a commercial day. But unfortunately, its primary purpose is making money, not honoring our mothers.

I'm not very materialistic, Lord. I don't have to have expensive gifts like jewelry. But I would like my children to show me some gratitude; a thoughtful card would be lovely. The world tells me I deserve this! When I don't get what I *expect*, I get upset and hurt! I don't feel appreciated and loved.

I know you're not materialistic, and your children should show you gratitude and honor you. But why do you need to feel appreciated by them?

I guess because when I receive appreciation from them, it validates my worth. It makes me feel I'm valuable and essential. So, Mother's Day is like a "Thank you, Mom! You're wonderful!"

But if you depend on others to validate your worth, that's not healthy. Remember a long time ago, I told you that "my grace is sufficient" when you were in so much pain, all day and all night for about seven months?

I'll never forget that time! I didn't like your answer because I wanted you to heal me.

I know you did, but I had other plans for you. I wanted you to experience the depth of my love. I wanted to sit by your side and help you fall asleep. I wanted our relationship to be even closer than it was before.

Yes, those were difficult and unbearable days! I understand what you mean. Because of that painful experience, I got closer to you like never before! Even though the pain was excruciating, being so close to you was priceless and comforting. I got to know you more, Lord! After that experience, now our time together is more meaningful.

Yes! You couldn't do anything to help yourself get better or take the pain away. All you could do was lie on your bed. You felt helpless. That's when you came to me with a humble heart. You started to understand my love for you! You are so valuable and precious to me. Don't allow the world to tell you that you're not valuable because you're not showered with gifts. Don't forget how much *I value and love you.*

You're right, Lord. Thank you for reminding me that I don't need others to praise me for feeling valuable or worthy because you love me. I'm important to you! The world's expectations shouldn't matter to me. I'm slowly gaining strength and wholeness in myself as I understand how much you love me. As I live with you, seek you every morning, and sit beside you, I'm slowly grasping the *depth of your love* and *grace* and the *belief* you have in me.

I'm sorry, Lord, I forget how much you love me.

Yes. I love you, my precious daughter!

(After my children realized that they had forgotten about Mother's Day, they felt terrible. So, each one of them bought dinner during that week instead of going out to dinner on Sunday. They know I don't like cooking, so those were great gifts!

The following year on Mother's Day, I didn't have worldly thoughts like the previous year. I didn't have any expectations of gifts or praise. So, I wasn't disappointed when nothing happened. God reminded me that my children love me because, throughout the year, they say thank you to me for the things I've done for them. He told me that those precious words are more meaningful because they're genuine and not prompted by a day designated for moms on Mother's Day. So, I smiled and felt content. He was right.

However, like the previous year, during the week of Mother's Day, each child bought dinner for the family, so I didn't have to cook. So, Mother's Day felt like it lasted the entire week! That was better than gifts!

Now it has become a new family tradition; we don't go out to a fancy restaurant on Mother's Day or give gifts, but eat at home all week with food I didn't cook! I LOVE THAT!)

God, you taught me to examine my expectations. Are they the world's expectations or God's expectations?

If they're the world's expectations, I'll get upset and disappointed. If they're your expectations, I'll be at peace and contentment.

Reflections:

- What worldly expectations upset you when they aren't fulfilled?
- When was the last time you let the Lord show you how much he loves you?

Good and Faithful Servant

While they were listening to this, he went on to tell them a parable, because he was near Jerusalem and the people thought that the kingdom of God was going to appear at once. He said: "A man of noble birth went to a distant country to have himself appointed king and then to return. So he called ten of his servants and gave them ten minas. 'Put this money to work,' he said, 'until I come back.' But his subjects hated him and sent a delegation after him to say, 'We don't want this man to be our king.' He was made king, however, and returned home. Then he sent for the servants to whom he had given the money, in order to find out what they had gained with it. The first one came and said, 'Sir, your mina has earned ten more.' 'Well done, my good servant!' his master replied. 'Because you have been trustworthy in a very small matter, take charge of ten cities.' The second came and said, 'Sir, your mina has earned five more.' His master answered, 'You take charge of five cities.' Then another servant came and said, 'Sir, here is your mina; I have kept it laid away in a piece of cloth. I was afraid of you, because you are a hard man. You take out what you did not put in and reap what you did not sow.' His master replied, 'I will judge you by your own words, you wicked servant! You knew, did you, that I am a hard man, taking out what I did not put in and reaping what I did not sow? Why then didn't you put my money on deposit so that when I came back, I could have collected it with interest?' Then he said to those standing by, 'Take his mina away from him and give it to the one who has ten minas.' 'Sir,' they said, 'he already has ten!' He replied, 'I tell you that to everyone who has, more will be given, but as for the one who has nothing, even what they have will be taken away. But those enemies of mine who did not want me to be king over them—bring them here and kill them in front of me.'" (Luke 19:11-27, NIV).

Lord, many pastors have preached on this parable and told us to do things for you. When we do, we will be called your good and faithful servants. But I don't think I'm a good and faithful servant because I keep making mistakes, and sometimes I have a terrible attitude. Even though you've helped me through hard times, and I've grown from them, I don't like going through them. I don't want to grow and be a mature Christian. See, my attitude is terrible, Lord. This isn't the attitude of a good servant.

I understand. Some of your hardships have been very difficult, hurtful, and painful. Nobody wants pain and suffering. When your bad attitude surfaces, you're feeling overwhelmed. When this happens, I want you to rest in me and get refreshed. Jesus needed to be alone with me and get refreshed too. If you don't, your spiritual body will weaken. Satan tries to cast doubt and tells you you're not a good servant for me. I want you to stop him and shout, "In the Name of the Lord Jesus Christ, get out of here!" Claim my power over him! He will flee when he hears my name and see that you're strengthened with my power!

You're right, Lord. When I'm tired and overwhelmed, Satan puts thoughts of fear and negativity in me. When these thoughts come, I will seek your protection and guidance.

Yes, I am always here for you. I will protect you, guide you, and help you change your attitude! You don't always have a bad attitude. It pops up once in a while, but I'm here to help you through that.

The passage makes you feel you need to be a perfect servant, like giving me ten minas for the one mina given. But it doesn't say perfect servant; it says "good and faithful servant." So I don't expect perfect servants.

Being a "good servant" is when you're serving me with a good heart. I see your motives. I know if they're pure or for selfish ambition.

Making mistakes is okay. What's important is when you're aware of your mistakes, you fix them or learn from them.

Now a "faithful servant" believes in me and comes to me for wisdom and guidance. This faithful servant wants to spend time with me.

I'm grateful that you look at my heart and don't expect perfection. But Lord, sometimes I'm afraid to do things for you. I don't feel I'm good enough or capable. I know I shouldn't be scared. I'm sorry, Lord.

Why are you afraid? I'm always here for you. I will help you when you're in the deep valleys. I will never leave you. I will be by your side and guide you.

Remember when I asked you to teach a Sunday school class for women? You were scared and didn't feel capable because you lacked knowledge. What did I tell you back then?

You said I didn't have to know everything about the Bible. I just needed to be a facilitator and be honest when I didn't know something. You wanted me to be transparent so they would be comfortable sharing. I remember thinking, "I can talk and be honest." So, I started the class.

It was scary for you to teach women because you usually taught the little ones. This was challenging for you, but I was with you every step of the way. I was guiding you and giving you wisdom. You thought this would be a hard time in your life, but you have cherished memories when you look back at that class! You got so close to those ladies. You loved them so much! Unfortunately, so many of them have passed away since they were older than you, but you will see them again in heaven. So why are you afraid? When I am with you, you have nothing to fear!

You're right. I know I shouldn't be afraid. You have helped me walk through many valleys, and the outcome has been victorious like that women's class. Thank you for reminding me of your love and your promise that you will never leave me.

When you think back to that women's class, what happened while you were leading that women's class?

When I was facilitating that class, I continually sought your help because I didn't know everything. Finally, when the class finished, I realized my faith grew because I needed to trust you and not me!

So, you're saying, when you're scared, your faith grows because you're relying on me. I make you more faithful. See, you're becoming a faithful servant.

When you're a faithful servant, what happens next?

You help me do things as I'm being your vessel. You give me wisdom and guide me on the next adventure.

Yes, you become more fruitful. You see blessings around you. You learned valuable lessons from leading that women's class! As you would say, "It was sooo good, Lord!"

Yes, Lord! It was the beginning of leading other adult classes. I love seeing the fruit or the blessings as I obey you.

And when you're fruitful, you become humble. You see my power! I see your tears flow from your eyes! So let's put this together in *your words* so you can recite them to yourself.

> **When I'm scared, you make me faithful.**
> **When I'm faithful, you make me fruitful.**
> **When I'm fruitful, you make me humble.**

That's so good, Lord! Thank you for showing me that I can be your good and faithful, humble servant *as long as you're beside me.* And it's okay to be scared as long as I *seek* you, *listen* to you, and *obey* you. You are here for me.

Yes! I am always here for you and ready to help you. I see your servant's heart.

(*As I was reviewing this devotion, I kept thinking, I thought the servants were given five talents, three talents, and one talent. Was I wrong in my recollection? So, I looked it up and found that this parable was also written in Matthew 25:14-30. So, I asked the Lord about it.*)

Lord, I'm confused about how the two parables are very similar yet different in each servant's gift. Did I mishear you about what you wanted me to learn?

I understand your confusion. One says "minas" while the other says "talents." It's okay to search for interpretations, but the lesson I wanted you to learn stays the same from either passage.

(*So, I looked up some interpretations. The verses are similar but not exact. In Matthew, it does say five talents, three talents, and one talent. One interpretation says: The Parable of the Talents focuses on our faithful service with what we've been given. The Parable of the Minas focuses on our testimony as a believer in our everyday life. Each of us is given the same "mina," which is the gift of salvation. So, I continued our conversation.*)

https://www.versebyverseministry.org/bible-answers/ explaining-talents-vs-minas

Okay, I understand the difference between the two passages. Yet, it doesn't matter because your lesson focused on my misconception of a "good and faithful servant."

Yes. If you focus on being a good and faithful servant, you will be focusing on both aspects of the passages. Faithfully serving me with what I've given you and sharing your testimony as a believer.

Thank you, Lord, for clarifying and confirming your lesson for me.

Reflections:

- I know that one day God will ask us, "What have you done for me with the gift of salvation and the abilities I gave you?" What will your response be?
- If you aren't aware of your God-given talents and abilities, won't you ask God to reveal them to you?

No Obstacles

"On the first day of the week, very early in the morning, the women took the spices they had prepared and went to the tomb. They found the stone rolled away from the tomb, but when they entered, they did not find the body of the Lord Jesus" (Luke 24:1-3, NIV).

You've read this and heard this part many times. This time, I want you to focus on the women.

Okay, the women took the spices to prepare Jesus' body. I remember that part.

I want you to continue reading verse 2, *"They found the stone rolled away from the tomb."*

Stop there and listen.

Remember the verses Luke 23:55-56 (NIV) *"...The women who had come with Jesus from Galilee followed Joseph and saw the tomb and how his body was laid in it. Then they went home and prepared spices and perfumes. But they rested on the Sabbath in obedience to the commandment."*?

Yup.

These verses show that they saw the tomb, and his body was laid inside by Joseph of Arimathea. They saw the huge stone that closed it. How did they think they were going to move it? Maybe they could ask the guards. What if the guards said "No"? That would make sense because their job was to guard the tomb. The officials didn't want the disciples to take Jesus' body. If the disciples did, they would claim that Jesus was alive since his body wasn't there.

The guards were there for a purpose! It's reasonable to assume the guards wouldn't move the enormous stone.

Maybe they thought the guards would move the stone since they were women. Then, they could innocently explain that they wished to put the spices on his body.

That's a possibility, but the *stone* wasn't an obstacle for them at all. The women didn't think about how they were going to move the stone. All they cared about was putting the spices on his body because that was their custom. They *needed* to do that because they loved Jesus. Their focus was on love and not obstacles, like a stone.

I have stones in front of me, huh, Lord? Those women didn't make excuses like me. They had a task to do for you! They didn't question or worry. Instead, they just went forward and onward to the tomb!

Yes, they went ahead without worrying because they had faith. When I give you a task, I will take care of every detail to help you complete your task. So, don't worry about the obstacles.

Even if the obstacle is the "unwillingness to submit" to you, Lord? I want everyone to love you, Lord, and follow you. I see the struggles they're going through, and you're the answer, but I can't force them to submit to you. I know you've told me to "wait and pray," but it's getting hard. The obstacle of "unwillingness to submit" is like that massive stone before them. But like the women, I will trust you to take care of everything and go forward with you. Please give me your wisdom to help others.

I know and see your tears for them. I want you to be available to them. You need to listen and give encouragement. Try not to advise unless they ask you. Listening is the key.

Yes, Lord.

Reflections:

- Are you focusing on an obstacle that seems to be preventing you from obeying God?
- Trust God to take care of the obstacle(s) and details as you do what he's asked you to do.

A Threenager in Traffic

(My three-year-old and I usually go driving around 9:30 a.m. But today was early in the morning, about 7 a.m. Needless to say, there was the usual morning traffic! I was driving for quite a while and going very slow when he shouted at me.)

"GO FASTER!"

"I can't because there are a lot of cars. This is what you call 'traffic.'"

"I go out and push cars!"

"What?" *(I was smiling at his response because at first, it was cute. But then...)*

"I said, 'Go faster!'"

"I told you I can't. Look, there are a lot of cars in front of me, so I have to drive slowly."

(Then I stopped because the other vehicles stopped.).

He yelled, "Go now!"

(I was so shocked at the negative comments or commands he was giving me! I wasn't smiling anymore! I was getting more annoyed by the minute. I wanted to yell at him too, but I knew that wouldn't help him understand. So, I stopped responding to his commands.

That's when God said...)

I know he's irritating you, and you're getting upset because you can't do anything to stop his negative attitude. I understand that. It's okay if he's complaining. Let him say what he needs to say. You're right about not responding to him. As he complains, let's talk. I want to teach you something. I know this is obvious, but I want you to look straight ahead. Tell me what you see.

I see a lot of cars moving slowly.

Each car represents a person and their life. So, you're looking at life right now. Everyone is driving or going somewhere because life is about moving. This is your life too. You're on my path, and you're moving slowly.

Yup, this is irritating, though. You know I don't have patience!

I know it's difficult for you to move slowly and wait. You prefer moving quickly, and you love efficiency. But I want you to stay on course. Keep going straight, and *don't* detour. I know it's tempting to go another way, but it will take you longer to get there if you do.

(Then, my three-year-old interrupted our conversation.)

"Stop the car and carry me!"

I know you want to stop because he'll stop complaining, but don't stop the car. He understands explanations, so explain why stopping the car and carrying him will not help him get home faster.

You're right, Lord. Okay.

"Sweetie, do you remember the day I stopped the car and turned off the road to clean your nose? You sneezed and had a lot of boogers coming out, so I needed to clean you up. But when I did that, it took us longer to get home. I had to drive farther to get back onto the freeway. I know it's hard, but you just need to wait and relax. I don't like this waiting either. Now try to close your eyes and go back to sleep. I know you're tired."

(To my amazement, he calmed down a bit and stopped his yelling. Finally, he closed his eyes and tried to sleep.)

Oh, thank you, Lord, for the advice about explaining things to him. I think he likes explanations because we're treating him like an adult, and he understands.

He's calmed down a bit so let's continue our conversation. Like you just told him, "detours" feel like wasted time. In life, detours are when the world distracts you. It's when you're doing things that aren't of value to me. It hurts me when you get so busy that you forget about *me*!

I'm sorry, Lord, and you're right. When I'm busy, I forget to sit before you and just listen to you. When things are hectic, that's when I should be seeking your advice and guidance even more. Instead, I tend to complain more to you.

It's okay to complain to me like he is complaining to you. But I want you to stay on track and stay focused on *me*. I know it's hard to wait and move slowly, but I have an excellent plan ahead. You just have to stay on course and keep moving forward with me, especially when you notice that events or problems are moving slowly.

Yes, that's my biggest problem, Lord. I'm impatient and don't like to wait.

Think about it. Can he see your final destination?

No, he can't see it. Nothing looks familiar to him. He doesn't see any landmarks that tell him we're close.

He doesn't know where he is and doesn't know how long he will wait. That's why he's also upset. It's not just the waiting, but it's the unknown of *how long* this will take. Does that sound familiar?

Yup, that describes me too. My little "threenager" is impatient and demanding, just like me!

But Lord, if you told me the length of time I would need to wait, I'd probably get more upset. I would be counting the days and getting more anxious as the days or years went by.

Yes, now you understand me more. You would be focusing on the number of days instead of focusing on me. You wouldn't have the peace that I want to give you. Instead, you would be filled with anxiety. You told your three-year-old to trust you, wait and relax.

Uh-huh.

Isn't that what I tell you too? You can't see ahead and don't know my exact plans or what path I'm going to take you on, but *trust* me. I have never steered you wrong. I want you to stay on track and keep focused on me by spending time with me. Then you can relax in my arms and not worry. You can't do anything to make things go faster. So, let's enjoy this time together. It will help you pass the time away as you drive, both in traffic and in life.

Wow, Lord, you're so good! I can't believe you turned this irritating situation into a beautiful lesson I need to share.

> I can't see ahead, so I'll keep trusting God.
> I'll keep my focus on Him and stay on His path.
> He will get me home and where I need to be.

(As we continued driving, we got closer to our destination, so I pointed out familiar landmarks to reassure him that we were almost there. To my surprise, he didn't stop complaining. In fact, he was more insistent about

going faster because he couldn't wait to get there. I smiled because I'm like that too. When I see God's plan coming together, I get excited and happy, and I want Him to hurry up.)

Oh Lord, I LOVE your illustrations! I remember your lessons more when you teach me in real-life situations. You're so incredible, God. Thank you, Lord! You never cease to amaze me!

Reflections:

- What kind of "traffic" do you have to deal with?
- What detours are you taking? When have you taken your eyes off of God because you were focused on your circumstances?
- How can you get back on the right course and trust God?

Be My Vessel

"On the third day, a wedding took place at Cana in Galilee. Jesus' mother was there, and Jesus and his disciples had also been invited to the wedding. When the wine was gone, Jesus' mother said to him, 'They have no more wine.' 'Woman, why do you involve me?' Jesus replied. 'My hour has not yet come.' His mother said to the servants, 'Do whatever he tells you.' Nearby stood six stone water jars, the kind used by the Jews for ceremonial washing, each holding from twenty to thirty gallons Jesus said to the servants, 'Fill the jars with water'; so they filled them to the brim. Then he told them, 'Now draw some out and take it to the master of the banquet.' They did so, and the master of the banquet tasted the water that had been turned into wine. He did not realize where it had come from, though the servants who had drawn the water knew. Then he called the bridegroom aside and said, 'Everyone brings out the choice wine first and then the cheaper wine after the guests have had too much to drink, but you have saved the best till now.' What Jesus did here in Cana of Galilee was the first of the signs through which he revealed his glory, and his disciples believed in him." (John 2:1-11, NIV).

I love Mary. She's bold and caring! She understands the embarrassment the young couple must feel. That's why she insists that Jesus helps the couple.

No, she doesn't insist that he help. Reread it from Mary's perspective and obedient heart.

Oh man, Lord! You're right! Since I tend to want my way and would be bold about it, I first read this from my selfish perspective. Thank you, Lord, for telling me to look at the situation through Mary's eyes.

I'm so embarrassed but grateful you opened my eyes to the truth and stopped me from viewing others from my point of view.

Even though Jesus tells her my time has not come, she tells the servants, "Do whatever he tells you." So she's telling him to do *whatever God tells him to do.*

Yes, she is! If I didn't want Jesus to perform the miracle, I would have told him not to. He would have told the servants not to do anything. The servants would still be following what Mary said to them.

Mary understood what her words meant. This conversation is a glimpse of their mother and son relationship. Mary is a faithful and obedient servant. She knows that Jesus is the Son of God and can't tell him what to do. So even though it appears she's telling him to perform a miracle, she is submitting to My will as she says, *"Do whatever he tells you."*

Now slowly reread the verses and notice what's *nearby.*

Verse 6 says, *"Nearby stood six stone water jars..."*

Those water jars are gigantic and capable of holding 20-30 gallons. Do you see how they're just there? They're ready to be used.

You want me to be like those jars and always be ready, huh? You want me to be your vessel with an open and loving heart.

Yes. To provide "wine for the couple," the servants needed something to hold the new wine. Remember the boy with the fish and loaves of bread? Something was there to use to multiply and feed the people. Be my vessel that's ready to be used at any time. Be available!

Yes, Lord!

Reflections:

- Are you submitting to God's Will like Mary did, or do you want things your way?
- How can you be available and ready to be used by God?
- How can you remind yourself to look at things from different perspectives?

Talk with Me like the Woman at the Well

When a Samaritan woman came to draw water, Jesus said to her, "Will you give me a drink?" (His disciples had gone into the town to buy food.)

The Samaritan woman said to him, "You are a Jew and I am a Samaritan woman. How can you ask me for a drink?" (For Jews do not associate with Samaritans.)

Jesus answered her, "If you knew the gift of God and who it is that asks you for a drink, you would have asked him, and he would have given you living water."

"Sir," the woman said, "you have nothing to draw with, and the well is deep. Where can you get this living water? Are you greater than our father Jacob, who gave us the well and drank from it himself, as did also his sons and his livestock?"

Jesus answered, "Everyone who drinks this water will be thirsty again, but whoever drinks the water I give them will never thirst. Indeed, the water I give them will become in them a spring of water welling up to eternal life."

The woman said to him, "Sir, give me this water so that I won't get thirsty and have to keep coming here to draw water."

He told her, "Go, call your husband, and come back."

"I have no husband," she replied.

Jesus said to her, "You are right when you say you have no husband. The fact is, you have had five husbands, and the man you now have is not your husband. What you have just said is quite true."

"Sir," the woman said, "I can see that you are a prophet. Our ancestors worshiped on this mountain, but you Jews claim that the place where we must worship is in Jerusalem."

"Woman," Jesus replied, "believe me, a time is coming when you will worship the Father neither on this mountain nor in Jerusalem. You Samaritans worship what you do not know; we worship what we do know, for salvation is from the Jews. Yet a time is coming and has now come when the true worshipers will worship the Father in the Spirit and in truth, for they are the kind of worshipers the Father seeks. God is Spirit, and his worshipers must worship in the Spirit and in truth."

The woman said, "I know that Messiah" (called Christ) "is coming. When he comes, he will explain everything to us."

Then, Jesus declared, "I, the one speaking to you—I am he." (John 4:7-26, NIV)

Do you see how long the conversation is?

Yes, I'm shocked.

What does that tell you about me?

Huh?

This extended conversation is showing you that I value talking with you and with my children.

Yes, I'm so glad you enjoy talking with me. These conversations help me get closer to you, Lord.

Yes, I'm pleased that we talk together too. Now, what is this passage all about?

The Samaritan woman focuses on the actual water from the well, but Jesus is talking about another type of water—his living water. She's confused, so she keeps talking and asking him questions. As they talk, she realizes he's a prophet. He even tells her that he's the Messiah in verse 26. *"I am he.'"*

Yes, she is starting to understand Jesus because she keeps talking and asking questions. This is an example of *genuinely seeking God*. Because she is searching or asking, the *truth* is revealed to her. Jesus tells her he's the Messiah. Did you understand that?

I think I do. When I talk and ask you questions, I'm *seeking you.*

Yes, I'm pleased when you seek me. But, when you do, I reveal the truth to you and open your eyes.

Oh, that's good, God! I love it when you show me something else in a passage or story I've heard before. Okay, "Seeking God" is talking and asking questions. You want us to just have a conversation with you, like what we're doing right now. Thank you, Lord, that you want to talk with me, listen to me, and tell me the truth about what I need to do.

Yes. Now continue reading John 4:39-42.

> *"Many of the Samaritans from that town believed in him because of the woman's testimony, 'He told me everything I ever did.' So, when the Samaritans came to him, they urged him to stay with them, and he stayed two days. And because of his words, many more became believers. They said to the woman, 'We no longer believe just because of what you said; now we have heard for*

ourselves, and we know that this man really is the Savior of the world'" (John 4:39-42, NIV).

I want you to summarize what occurred.

The people in the town came to hear Jesus because of *her* testimony. That's interesting because they looked down upon her before. That's why she got water later in the day to avoid their gossiping.

Yes, she was ashamed of her behavior.

But now I want you to look at verse 42 again.

> *"They said to the woman, 'We no longer believe just because of what you said; now we have heard for ourselves, and we know that this man really is the Savior of the world.'"*

They didn't believe her because of what she said. They believed Jesus because they heard him for themselves. You can't get close to me because of what someone else says to you or what that person learned from the Bible. You have to *experience Christ* for yourself! You have to *spend time with me*!

Oh, that's so good, God! I love it when you show me a hidden gem! It's always been there, but I didn't see it before! I need to experience God for myself! I need to spend time with you and listen.

Yes! Remember these verses.

> *"Come close to God, and God will come close to you. Wash your hands, you sinners; purify your hearts, for your loyalty, is divided between God and the world"* (James 4:8, NIV, emphasis added).

> *"Be still, and know that I am God. I will be exalted among the nations. I will be exalted in the earth!"* (Psalms 46:10, NIV).

Reflections:

- How are you seeking God?
- Are you learning about God from someone else or from God himself?
- How has God shown you that he knows you?
- Would you like to have a conversation with God?

Jesus Appears Three Times

Now Mary stood outside the tomb crying. As she wept, she bent over to look into the tomb and saw two angels in white, seated where Jesus' body had been, one at the head and the other at the foot. They asked her, "Woman, why are you crying?"

"They have taken my Lord away," she said, "and I don't know where they have put him."

At this, she turned around and saw Jesus standing there, but she did not realize that it was Jesus. He asked her, "Woman, why are you crying? Who is it you are looking for?"

Thinking he was the gardener, she said, "Sir, if you have carried him away, tell me where you have put him, and I will get him."

Jesus said to her, "Mary."

She turned toward him and cried out in Aramaic, "Rabboni!" (which means "Teacher").

Jesus said, "Do not hold on to me, for I have not yet ascended to the Father. Go instead to my brothers and tell them, 'I am ascending to my Father and your Father, to my God and your God.'" Mary Magdalene went to the disciples with the news: "I have seen the Lord!" And she told them that he had said these things to her.

On the evening of that first day of the week, when the disciples were together, with the doors locked for fear of the Jewish leaders, Jesus came and stood among them and said, "Peace be with you!" After he said this, he showed them his hands and side. The disciples were overjoyed when they saw the Lord. Again, Jesus said,

*"Peace be with you! As the Father has sent me, I am sending you."
And with that, he breathed on them and said, "Receive the Holy
Spirit. If you forgive anyone's sins, their sins are forgiven; if you
do not forgive them, they are not forgiven."*

*Now Thomas (also known as Didymus), one of the Twelve, was
not with the disciples when Jesus came. So the other disciples told
him, "We have seen the Lord!"*

*But he said to them, "Unless I see the nail marks in his hands
and put my finger where the nails were, and put my hand into
his side, I will not believe."*

*A week later, his disciples were in the house again, and Thomas
was with them. Though the doors were locked, Jesus came and
stood among them and said, "Peace be with you!" Then he said
to Thomas, "Put your finger here; see my hands. Reach out your
hand and put it into my side. Stop doubting and believe."*

Thomas said to him, "My Lord and my God!"

*Then Jesus told him, "Because you have seen me, you have believed;
blessed are those who have not seen and yet have believed."* John
20:11-29 (NIV)

Reread and write down who Jesus appears to.

Jesus appears to Mary.

Jesus appears to the disciples.

Jesus appears to Thomas.

**Now let's look at each encounter closely. First, what did I tell Mary
in verse 17?**

You told Mary, *"...don't hold onto me, for I have not yet ascended to the Father."*

She was holding on to me because she didn't want me to leave again. She's remembering the past. I don't want you to hold onto the past, either. Instead, I want you to look ahead and go forward, just like Mary went to the disciples. I know it's hard to let go of the past, but I'm with you every step of the way.

What did I give the disciples in verse 22?

You gave the disciples, *"... the Holy Spirit."* The Holy Spirit is your power and my guidance and wisdom. Without him, I can't have a close relationship with you.

Yes, you need the Holy Spirit! He can be with you all the time, unlike Jesus, when he was on earth. You can always rely on Him. He is there for you, every day and every minute.

Now, what did I do for Thomas in verse 27?

It says, *"Put your finger here; see my hands. Reach out your hand and put it into my side. Stop doubting and believe."* You knew Thomas was doubting, so you helped him with his unbelief. He needed to see and touch your hands.

Yes. I know sometimes you want to see and touch me. But your faith is greater. Remember verse 29, *"... blessed are those who have not seen and yet have believed."* That describes you and a multitude of my children. I'm so pleased with my faithful servants. Yet, I know there are times when you feel exactly like Thomas. I understand, but I don't want you to doubt or hesitate like him. Instead, I want you to believe and do what I say! As a result, your faith will be greater and strengthened.

Wow, Lord, three things we all *need to do* in our Christian walk. I never saw how all three of these incidents were connected.

Mary: Let go of the past and move ahead with God.

Disciples: Ask the Holy Spirit for wisdom and guidance.

Thomas: Stop doubting. Believe, trust, and obey God.

(With the help of the Holy Spirit, we can let go of the past, move ahead with God, stop our doubting, and replace it with believing, trusting, and obeying God. It's like an Oreo, where the center is the best part, and without it, the whole cookie wouldn't taste good! By having the Holy Spirit in the middle of our Christian walk, He can guide every decision, making our life sweeter and GOOD!)

Reflections:

- What area(s) in your Christian walk does God want you to focus on?
  o Letting go of the past and moving ahead with God
  o Seeking the Holy Spirit for wisdom and guidance
  o Stopping your doubts. Instead, believe, trust and obey Him.

Don't Look Back; Go Forward

Oh man, God, I messed up! I was focusing on something else, so I drove the wrong way! Good grief! I guess that's what happens when I'm not paying attention and getting distracted. But I was focusing on a song about *you*, Lord.

Yes, but even spending time with me can be a distraction or a way to avoid something. I knew this would teach you something, so I let you get distracted.

I can't believe I did that, Lord. But I'm glad I stopped and parked in the shopping center. Thank you for calming me down and helping me to refocus. You said I need to share about you but in a different way. Okay...I don't understand, but I will trust you.

Okay, Lord, I need to fix this. I'm going back to where I was and taking the correct entrance to get on the freeway.

(I started driving for a bit, and I missed the exit again!)

I can't believe I messed up like that *again!* I've never done that before. I need to get back to where I was! Ugh!

NO! Slow down a bit and keep driving. Now quick, take this next exit! You can still get on it since nobody is behind you.

Huh?

Quickly, do it! Keep driving.

Okay. Oh, I see where I am. I know where to go now. But man, Lord, what's the matter with me? That's the second time I missed an exit! I've never missed an off-ramp *twice*! Thank you for helping me and keeping me safe. I feel stupid!

Good, you're back on track. Now look at where you are and listen carefully. You thought going back to where you were or where you started was the correct path. However, I wanted you to continue forward with me, even though you were unsure because nothing looked familiar. I knew there was another way to get to your destination instead of backtracking.

Sometimes in life, you feel like you've failed. For example, you think you're not following me because your past mistakes stop you from believing in me. You feel like you "missed the boat," and your life is a mess or mediocre.

Yup.

So, I want you to lean in and listen now. Then, when you make mistakes, I want you to go forward with me! I know another way for you to get to the same destination. Don't focus on your past pains or mistakes. Just go forward with me, and trust me!

Oh, man Lord! That's a good illustration. This irritating but silly mistake will help me remember your essential lesson of 'not looking back to my past. So instead, I will go forward with you.

This reminds me of past hurt. Someone important in my life said hurtful words to me. That person made me feel unworthy and belittled. I wasn't needed and was blamed for other things that were going wrong. I remember crying out to you, Lord! I was so shocked and hurt! But you told me to forgive that person. I couldn't. It took me a long time to forgive, but with your help, I did. You reminded me that I have faults too, and that person cares for me despite them, so I should do the same and forgive.

Yes, I remember that time. You tried rationalizing the situation and even buried it for a time. You finally realized that you had to face the hurt and deal with it because it held you back from growing with me. You needed to forgive.

Yes, Lord. I finally forgave that person with your love and guidance.

Because you forgave, you were able to let go of the painful and hurtful past that was caused. You became free to go forward. A tremendous burden was lifted off your shoulders!

Yes, Lord!

I've also told you not to rely on others to make you feel valuable or worthy. You weren't aware of it at the time, but you depended on that person to make you feel valuable. So instead, I want you to look at my words in the Bible or the promises I have given you.

"For we are God's handiwork, created in Christ Jesus to do good works, which God prepared in advance for us to do" (Ephesians 2:10, NIV).

I created you! You are my handiwork! I don't make mistakes!

> *"What is the price of two sparrows—one copper coin? But not a single sparrow can fall to the ground without your Father knowing it. And the very hairs on your head are all numbered. So don't be afraid; you are more valuable to God than a whole flock of sparrows"* (Matthew 10:29-31, NLT).

You are more valuable to me than the sparrows! I know everything about you. You are so precious to me!

Thank you, Lord, for freeing me of my painful past and helping me go forward with you. I need to stop seeking approval from others but remember that I am valuable, and I am your handiwork.

(I finally arrived at home, and God showed me some verses.)

Remember my words…

> *"Forget the former things; do not dwell on the past. See, I am doing a new thing! Now it springs up; do you not perceive it? I am making a way in the wilderness & streams in the wasteland"* (Isaiah 43:18-19, NIV).

> *"Then he will say to those on his left, 'Depart from me, you who are cursed, into the eternal fire prepared for the devil and his angels"* (Matthew 25:41, NIV).

When Satan tries to drag me down and burden me with my past hurts and mistakes, I will remember that verse and what his future will be. Thank you for reminding me that you are more powerful than the enemy. He's staying in hell, as planned! The enemy is already defeated because you have power over him! Amen!

Yes, the enemy is scared of his future. He wants to take as many people with him as he can.

Reflections:

- What's keeping you from moving forward with God? A past hurt? A past mistake? A grudge against someone?
- Don't rely on others to make you feel important. You are important! He created you!
- Review the verses or truths God has given you. Memorize one.

Goodness

*"For this very reason, make every effort to add to your faith good-
ness; and to goodness, knowledge; and to knowledge, self-control;
and to self-control, perseverance; and to perseverance, godliness; and to godliness, brotherly kindness; and to brotherly
kindness, love. For if you possess these qualities in increasing
measure, they will keep you from being ineffective and unpro-
ductive in your knowledge of our Lord Jesus Christ. But whoever does not have them is nearsighted and blind, forgetting
that they have been cleansed from their past sins. Therefore, my
brothers and sisters make every effort to confirm your calling
and election. For if you do these things, you will never stumble"*
(2 Peter 1:5-10, NIV).

I want to have these traits so I can be effective and productive for you.
However, there are so many traits. Which one do you want me to
focus on?

**I want you to focus on all of them, but let's look at them one at a
time. Today, we will focus on goodness.**

Okay.

What's goodness to you?

Goodness is being good or nice to others and thinking about others.

**Yes, but goodness is also thinking of the good *in* others, the good-
ness in that person. So, when you talk to people, think of that person's good qualities, like your friend that is hurting now. She is
intelligent, loving, compassionate, organized, kind, and has a great**

smile. So, when you listen to her, tell her about the good qualities she has.

Wow, Lord, I love that! It's enlightening, and you're so wise! Why am I shocked You are a wise God. Think of the good *in* people. You're right. When I do that, I'm showing goodness.

Yes, show my goodness to people. Seeing the good in people is part of my character, so when you do that, you share a part of me, showing love to that person.

This is more practical or easier for me to understand. The idea of goodness as being good to others seems vague because it encompasses many things. When something is unclear, people usually don't do it. It's easier to do when things are more specific. Thank you, Lord, for giving me detailed instructions.

Remember,

Goodness: see the good in others and tell them.

Reflections:

- Did this devotion make you think of someone in particular? Then make it a point to share with that person the good you see in them.
- Show "goodness" to yourself too. Think of the "good" in you! Then thank God for giving you those beautiful qualities!

Knowledge

"For this very reason, make every effort to add to your faith goodness; and to goodness, knowledge; and to knowledge, self-control; and to self-control, perseverance; and to perseverance, godliness; and to godliness, brotherly kindness; and to brotherly kindness, love. For if you possess these qualities in increasing measure, they will keep you from being ineffective and unproductive in your knowledge of our Lord Jesus Christ. But whoever does not have them is nearsighted and blind, forgetting that they have been cleansed from their past sins. Therefore, my brothers and sisters make every effort to confirm your calling and election. For if you do these things, you will never stumble."
2 Peter 1:5-10. (NIV)

Okay, Lord, you said to focus on each word per day. So today, we're looking at *knowledge*.

Yes, let's focus on knowledge. What does that mean to you?

It means learning about the knowledge of you, God. You want us to get to know you more by spending time with you.

Yes, that's true. However, it's about people too. I want you to get to know them better, not just spending time with them.

How?

When people are talking to you about their problems, I want you to *listen and understand* what they tell you because you don't always know the answer(s). Therefore, I want you to be supportive instead of giving advice. Acknowledge that you understood what was shared by repeating it back to the person. Then the other person can

correct any misconceptions if needed. After you have learned about the situation or problem, I will give you wisdom about responding. And remember what your husband said, "Don't give advice unless the person asks for it."

Okay, so "listen and understand." Help me to do this, Lord.

When I think about the *other person*'s good things, I will develop the goodness you want me to have. Then you want me to *listen and understand*, so I will gain more knowledge about that person. Finally, with more knowledge, you will give me the wisdom to help and be your vessel. You're so incredible, Lord! Thank you for showing me how I can apply these traits.

(The other day, my daughter called. She was upset about her job. So, I did what you said, "Listen and understand." I repeated the problem back in another analogy, so I understood the situation, and she knew I understood it. Then you gave me wisdom that I shared with her. She said, "You're right, mom.")

Thank you, Lord, for showing me how "*listening and understanding*" is how you give me knowledge and wisdom in everyday situations.

I'm glad you're applying what I say.
Remember...
> **Goodness: see the good in others and tell them.**

> **Knowledge: listen and understand, gain knowledge of the person, and God will give you the wisdom to respond.**

Reflections:

- Think of a time or situation when you applied this type of knowledge.
- When can you use this type of knowledge?

Self-Control

"For this very reason, make every effort to add to your faith goodness; and to goodness, knowledge; and to knowledge, self-control; and to self-control, perseverance; and to perseverance, godliness; and to godliness, brotherly kindness; and to brotherly kindness, love. For if you possess these qualities in increasing measure, they will keep you from being ineffective and unproductive in your knowledge of our Lord Jesus Christ. But whoever does not have them is nearsighted and blind, forgetting that they have been cleansed from their past sins. Therefore, my brothers and sisters make every effort to confirm your calling and election. For if you do these things, you will never stumble"
(2 Peter 1:5-10, NIV).

We're focusing on self-control today, Lord.

Yes. What does that mean to you?

It means to control my temper. Over the years, you've taught me that my temper is my selfishness because I want my way! I don't like that, But now I understand it. My temper problem is lessening because I'm working on surrendering my wants to you. Thank you for giving me consistent help and guidance in this area.

Yes, you're right about your temper and selfishness. I want you to control these traits, but I want you to focus on taking <u>control</u> of your body or taking <u>care</u> of your body. You started sleeping more because I told you to. Now you're getting seven hours of sleep, and your lungs are healing! I showed you these breathing exercises that will increase your lung capacity. Your health is just as important as your spiritual health. So, I want you to also stretch and do moderate exercises.

Okay, I understand. I need to take care of myself physically. Thank you for telling me about the breathing exercises through speakers I heard online. I will start stretching and exercising to improve my lungs.

Yes, you need to do those things. However, slow breathing will also lower your stress levels.

I know what you mean. The other day I felt some tension in my face, so I rested more, followed the breathing exercises, and it went away.

I'm pleased you're following my instructions. Remember, I created the body. So I know what it needs to function correctly. Now let's look at self-control from another perspective. It is also "controlling yourself so you won't meddle with my plans!" So let me take control or handle the situations that arise. Remember that wonderful phrase you found on a coaster you bought?

Yes! I love it and read it from time to time to remind me. Unfortunately, the author is unknown, but I know it's from you!

> Good Morning, this is God.
> I will be handling all your problems today.
> I will not need your help,
> So, have a good day.

So, I need to control what I can, like breathing slowly and taking care of my health. Then leave the rest of the day to you! You will take care of everything!

Remember...

Goodness: see the good in others and tell them.

Knowledge: listen and understand, gain knowledge of the person and God will give you the wisdom to respond.

Self-Control: control your breathing to take care of your health, take control of yourself, and don't meddle with my plans for you.

Reflections:

- Where do you need to have more self-control in your life?
- Where are you meddling and telling God your plans?

Perseverance

"For this very reason, make every effort to add to your faith good-ness; and to goodness, knowledge; and to knowledge, self-control; and to self-control, perseverance; and to perseverance, godli-ness; and to godliness, brotherly kindness; and to brotherly kindness, love. For if you possess these qualities in increasing measure, they will keep you from being ineffective and unpro-ductive in your knowledge of our Lord Jesus Christ. But who-ever does not have them is nearsighted and blind, forgetting that they have been cleansed from their past sins. Therefore, my brothers and sisters make every effort to confirm your calling and election. For if you do these things, you will never stumble" (2 Peter 1:5-10, NIV).

Today we're looking at perseverance.

What does that mean to you?

Perseverance means, *don't give up!* On the contrary, I should keep trying, especially when the task is challenging! It's a positive way of describing my *stubbornness*. I remember telling my parents, "I'm not stubborn. I have perseverance!"

Yes, and I remember that I'm the one that told you that!

Yes, thank you, Lord! That's when I started to understand that my weaknesses become strengths when I rely on you.

Perseverance doesn't only mean to keep trying. It also means to keep *seeking me* when times are difficult. So many people give up when they don't get their answers immediately. There are many

times my answer is "wait." People don't like waiting. This is when you need the perseverance to keep trusting me.

You told me to wait, and I'm still waiting. You're right. It's hard to keep seeking you. I need perseverance in seeking and trusting you, Lord. Oh, how I love it when you show me something new in your Word. Thank you, Lord!

Remember...

Goodness: see the good in others and tell them.

Knowledge: listen and understand, gain knowledge of the person and God will give you the wisdom to respond.

Self-Control: control your breathing to take care of your health take control of yourself, and don't meddle with my plans for you.

Perseverance: don't stop seeking and trusting the Lord.

Reflections:

- How does perseverance help you wait on the Lord?
- Why do you give up when waiting for an answer from God?
- Is there an area currently in your life where you need to persevere in seeking and trusting God?

Godliness

"For this very reason, make every effort to add to your faith good-ness; and to goodness, knowledge; and to knowledge, self-control; and to self-control, perseverance; and to perseverance, godli-ness; and to godliness, brotherly kindness; and to brotherly kindness, love. For if you possess these qualities in increasing measure, they will keep you from being ineffective and unpro-ductive in your knowledge of our Lord Jesus Christ. But who-ever does not have them is nearsighted and blind, forgetting that they have been cleansed from their past sins. Therefore, my brothers and sisters make every effort to confirm your calling and election. For if you do these things, you will never stumble" (2 Peter 1:5-10, NIV).

Now we're focusing on godliness.

What does that mean to you?

It means to be like you, Lord. Please show me something new.

Who am I?

You're love! Almighty! Powerful! Creator! You know everything! See everything!

Yes, I see everything that is happening now and what will happen. I see everything from my perspective. Do you understand that?

According to your perspective, there is a plan. Your timing is perfect. It's not too fast and not too slow. However, I want you to do things quickly, huh, Lord? I don't like waiting. But I get it. Your plan and timing is perfect. The only way!

Yes, so don't meddle or try to take matters into your own hands to make things go faster. Instead, keep waiting and praying, even though it's hard. Godliness is looking at things from my perspective, not yours. As you do this, you're becoming Christ-like.

Wow, Lord, your perspective! I never thought about godliness like that before. Help me to see things through your eyes, your point of view. You're right. When I do that, I understand your timing and plans a little better. I have more peace. Your plan is the only way! Thank you, Lord, for your wisdom!

Remember...

Goodness: see the good in others and tell them.

Knowledge: listen and understand, gain knowledge of the person and God will give you the wisdom to respond.

Self-Control: control your breathing to take care of your health take control of yourself, and don't meddle with my plans for you.

Perseverance: don't stop seeking and trusting the Lord.

Godliness: look at things from God's perspective.

Reflections:

- How can you look at things through God's eyes?
- Make it a point to look at one thing through God's eyes today. It can be small and simple.

Brotherly Kindness

"For this very reason, make every effort to add to your faith good-ness; and to goodness, knowledge; and to knowledge, self-control; and to self-control, perseverance; and to perseverance, godli-ness; and to godliness, brotherly kindness; and to brotherly kindness, love. For if you possess these qualities in increasing measure, they will keep you from being ineffective and unpro-ductive in your knowledge of our Lord Jesus Christ. But who-ever does not have them is nearsighted and blind, forgetting that they have been cleansed from their past sins. Therefore, my brothers and sisters make every effort to confirm your calling and election. For if you do these things, you will never stumble" (2 Peter 1:5-10, NIV).

Lord, this is exciting! I love how your explanation of your words are opening my eyes to understand more! What are you going to show me today about "brotherly kindness"?

What does that mean to you?

Kindness is being kind or friendly to others. But it says "brotherly kindness," so I'm thinking this type of kindness is when you're treating people like they're a part of your family. You protect, sacrifice, and gen-uinely care for family members.

Yes, brotherly kindness is treating someone like a family member. Kindness is what touches people's hearts. That's why you hear "random acts of kindness" instead of acts of goodness. Kindness is very close to *what love is*. When a person is touched by compassion, that person is more open to love, my godly love.

So, I need to treat others like they're a part of my family through my actions and words. Then they will feel this type of brotherly kindness.

Kindness can be a small gesture or a big one. But both must be done with a selfless attitude. People can tell when it's genuine. People will accept kindness from others, but it's hard to receive *love* because people are skeptical. They will wonder and question your motive.

Yeah, I get it. When I met someone, I showed kindness. After a while, we became friends and developed a bond of trust. Then that friend understood that I really cared. Being kind to one another is more important than I ever thought it was.

Yes. When you demonstrate acts of kindness toward others, people will feel your genuine love. They will feel like they're a part of your family. They feel loved by you. That's why the following word in the verse is *love*.

Thank you, Lord, for your wisdom!

Remember...

Goodness: see the good in others and tell them.

Knowledge: listen and understand, gain knowledge of the person and God will give you the wisdom to respond.

Self-Control: control your breathing to take care of your health take control of yourself, and don't meddle with my plans for you.

Perseverance: don't stop seeking and trusting the Lord.

Godliness: look at things from God's perspective.

Brotherly Kindness: do acts of genuine kindness toward others; opens people's hearts to God's love.

Reflections:

- When did you do an "act of genuine kindness" for someone?
- What "acts of genuine kindness" can you show to others today to open their heart to God?

Love

"For this very reason, make every effort to add to your faith goodness; and to goodness, knowledge; and to knowledge, self-control; and to self-control, perseverance; and to perseverance, godliness; and to godliness, brotherly kindness; and to brotherly kindness, love. For if you possess these qualities in increasing measure, they will keep you from being ineffective and unproductive in your knowledge of our Lord Jesus Christ. But whoever does not have them is nearsighted and blind, forgetting that they have been cleansed from their past sins. Therefore, my brothers and sisters make every effort to confirm your calling and election. For if you do these things, you will never stumble" (2 Peter 1:5-10, NIV).

The last one is "love."

What does that mean to you?

Love means you genuinely care about that person. It shows through your actions and words. You love the person despite their faults. You value and respect that person. Show me something new, Holy Spirit.

Okay, sit and be still. Clear your mind. Be quiet and listen. Let's go to the place in your mind where you sit amongst my creation. Come and be with me now.

Okay, Lord. As I walk, I see the majestic waterfall in the distance. I gaze up and see your wondrous rainbow. Then, I turn right and see the majestic trees and grass. I feel the cool breeze brush against my face as I walk slightly upward towards my tree. I sit and lean against it as it provides shade and peacefulness.

Where you're sitting is in "my love." There is peace, calmness, beauty, and no fears. You are content. You are resting in me. Feel my love. Understand my love for you.

Oh, Lord, yes. When I rest in you, I feel your love.

When you understand my love, then you can show my love.

Yes, Lord! That's so simple but true! As I spend time with you, I understand your love for me a little more every day. You fill me with your love. Then I can show your love to others. So, continue to fill me with your love through the Holy Spirit.

Thank you for showing me all of these words from your perspective. I will cherish them.

You took the time to stop and ask. I'm always here.

Thank you, Lord. Your Word is so precious! You give me new treasures every time I read your Word, even if I've read it before. There is something new, as long as I'm asking, seeking, and listening.

Yes!

Thank you, Lord, for your wisdom!

Remember...

Goodness: see the good in others and tell them.

Knowledge: listen and understand, gain knowledge of the person and God will give you the wisdom to respond.

Self-Control: control your breathing to take care of your health take control of yourself, and don't meddle with my plans for you.

Perseverance: don't stop seeking and trusting the Lord.

Godliness: look at things from God's perspective.

Brotherly Kindness: do acts of genuine kindness towards others; opens people's hearts to God's love.

Love: understand God's love, then you can show God's love.

Reflections:

- Go to the Lord. Sit and be still. Clear your mind. Be quiet and listen. Be with him.
- Now thank him for who he is.
- Feel his love embracing you.

Yucky Marinade

(I'm washing dishes. I'm just about to pour out the marinade from a container I had marinated the chicken in.)

STOP, don't pour it out! Listen to me!

Huh? Why?

Good, I got your attention. Now listen closely. Please look at it and tell me what you see.

I see dark, yucky, shoyu marinade. I also see some oily spots of fat from the chicken. Yuck.

This marinade represents your sins and all the yucky stuff inside your heart.

Ewww, gross!

Now put that marinade under the water faucet. Turn the water on, but not a full blast of water; a medium speed is good. I want you to wait and observe what's happening. I know it's tempting to dump the marinade because you want the container to be clean, but don't empty the container!

(So, I watch as the water fills the container and becomes full. Then the water starts overflowing.)

Now what?

I want you to observe. Look at the marinade and the water coming in. What's happening to it?

The water is going down into the bowl and kind of mixing the marinade. Hey, the marinade is slowly breaking up, and some of it is coming out! It's not as dark as before. I thought when the water was filling the bowl, the water would just overflow and runoff. That's cool, Lord.

The water is like me. I'm the *living water*. I want to pour my love into you every day and every minute to help you get rid of your sins of negativity, selfishness, and your hurts. But you have to allow me to give you my living water that's from the Holy Spirit. Now move the container away from the faucet. What happened?

Nothing happened. What am I suppose to see?

The marinade can't get out unless the water comes in. This is like you and me. I can't help you if you don't let me in; by reading my Word and spending time with me. The Holy Spirit is in you, but you're not allowing him to help you.

The water is still flowing out of the faucet, but *you* moved the container away from the water. That's like when you move away from me and take control of your life. Now move the container back under the faucet of water and watch! Keep watching and be patient! What do you see now?

The yucky marinade is almost gone, but I didn't dump it out! The water is overflowing.

When you start trusting me more, then you're able to start obeying me a little more. The more you follow me, the cleaner you become. Think about your temper when you were young. Compare it to now.

It's not as bad as it used to be.

The marinade or your temper is getting cleaner as you allow me in, and you surrender to me.

117

Oooh, I love visuals or object lessons! They help me remember more because I can see it!

So, keep me close to you, Lord. I want you to continually fill me with your love and power of the Holy Spirit. Sometimes I put in junk, huh, Lord?

Yes, you do. So, it's vital that my "overflowing water of love" is continually pouring into you! I am the living water. This water will continue to flow as you read and put my Word in your heart and mind. Keep listening to me.

Reflections:

- How are you allowing God to clean the yucky stuff out of your life? Are you seeking the power of the Holy Spirit?
- Did you move the container?
- Try this object lesson for yourself. You can color the water instead of using a yucky marinade.

Without Finding Fault

"If any of you lacks wisdom, he should ask God, who gives gen-
erously to all without finding fault, and it will be given to him"
(James 1:5, NIV).

What do you want me to focus on, Lord?

Slowly read the beginning phrase.

Okay. *"If any of you lacks wisdom..."*

Why did I write "If"? Look at it again.

"If any of you lacks wisdom..." I know I lack wisdom, so I don't understand why you used the word, "if."

I wrote "if" you lack wisdom because you need to *know* that you
lack my understanding. Many people think they're good and don't
need my knowledge.

Now I understand. The word "if" is a little word, but it's so vital.

When you realize you need wisdom from me, you're open to what
I'm going to say to you. Opening your heart to me is the first and
most crucial step.

So now, you understand the word "if." Now, let's go back and reread
the beginning phrase. There's another important word. Do you
see it?

"If any of you lacks wisdom..." It's wisdom, huh, Lord?

Yes. My wisdom is the most important thing I want for you. I didn't say love, faith, or hope, but wisdom. When you have wisdom, you'll understand my commandments more, and you'll naturally show my love to others. Your faith and hope will be stronger because you'll be trusting and obeying more when you ask for wisdom. Everything starts with my wisdom.

Yes, I understand. That makes sense, Lord. That's what I've always prayed for, especially when I became a mom. I didn't feel confident in being a good mom because I knew I was selfish. When I shared that with my mom, I was touched because she said that's what she prayed for when she became a mom. I remember tears flowing and feeling so close to my mom at that time. I still pray for your wisdom as a mom. You're right, Lord. Your wisdom is so important.

Okay, let's continue reading the verse.

It says, *"...he should ask God, who gives generously to all without finding fault..."*

When you come to me and humbly ask, I'll give you everything! I know what you need, and I'm pleased you're asking me.

I love the part *"without finding fault"* because you don't see my faults.

You're getting a little confused. The part *"gives generously to all without finding fault"* means you can't earn my love or wisdom. I delight in you when you come to me.

I see. You'll give me everything because you love me—that's what *"without finding fault"* really means. I don't have to do anything because you'll give it freely when I ask you. So, I can ask you for wisdom at any time, in any situation.

Yes, absolutely! You can't earn my love or wisdom. You just need to ask me. However, let's talk about what you said before about

not seeing your faults. I don't see them because you don't have any faults. I made you exactly the way I wanted you to be. You see your faults as your weaknesses, but I don't see it that way. Your flaws are a part of who you are. You *need them* to fulfill your potential and, more importantly, the specific purpose(s) that I created you for.

I never thought of my weaknesses like that. I've always heard comments like, "You have such a bad temper! You don't think before you speak!" So, I have always hated my weaknesses. But you're right. You've shown me how my weaknesses have helped many people. Because my personality is to speak first and think later, I have made many mistakes. So, you taught me to apologize. Since I still make mistakes, apologizing is part of who I am now.

My daughter told me once that adults usually don't apologize to their co-workers or friends. Parents have a hard time apologizing to their children too. She said she's learning to apologize by my example. When she shared this with me, my heart was so touched. I need my weaknesses to *fulfill my potential for you,* Lord! I never thought I'd ever say this, but thank you for my weaknesses!

Wow, Lord! You told me to reread James verse by verse instead of by sections. This is cool, Lord! I love it! This is exciting, Lord! You're going to show me the book of James in a *new* way! Aaah, I can't wait!

Reflections:

- Why do you need God's wisdom?
- How do you feel knowing that God created you perfectly, including your weaknesses, to complete your purpose for him?
- Ask him today for his wisdom and to use your perceived weaknesses for his purposes.

Blown and Tossed by the Wind

"But when he asks, he must believe and not doubt because he who doubts is like a wave of the sea, blown and tossed by the wind" (James 1:6, NIV).

This verse describes me! I ask you for things, but I doubt you, Lord.

I want you to look at the rest of the verse again. Pay attention and picture the *"wave of the sea, blown and tossed by the wind."*

I see that it's hard for the wave to go forward. It goes back and forth and in different directions when it's blown by the wind. The wind is an outside force.

Yes, the wind is your world of selfishness, temptations, and distractions. It stops you from going forward. Instead, it pulls you in a different direction and pushes you toward other distractions. That's when doubts enter your mind, allowing Satan to slip in negative thoughts, which push you away from me. Then you turn away from the path I know is best for you, and you start going in the wrong direction!

Yeah. At first, it seems okay because I'm relaxed with the wave, just moving a little and drifting along. Nothing appears wrong at first. It's like my doubts; they start small and ordinary.

Satan knows how to prey upon your thought process. He starts subtly like planting a seed of doubt, then telling you "it's normal to have some doubts. Everybody is like that." So, it's essential to be aware of what's happening. As you let the doubts grow, they turn into negative thoughts. When they do that, your mind will start spiraling downward. Satan wants you to get far away from me.

Oh Lord, protect me from life's distractions and doubting you. I want to stay on your path. That's easy to say, but it's hard for me to do! So how do I keep on track?

Remember the verse 2 Corinthians 10:5 (NIV), *"We demolish arguments and every pretension that sets itself up against the knowledge of God, and we take captive every thought to make it obedient to Christ."*

The first step is to be aware of your doubts, distractions, negative thoughts, and impure thoughts. Then, take hold of them with a firm grip and ask me for power from my Word and the Holy Spirit to overcome these thoughts. Like the verse says, you are taking the thought captive. This is a real battle in your thought life. I want you to continually come to me. I will protect you and guide you. So, keep close to me so you can hear my directions and stay on my path.

You're right, Lord. When I'm close to you, I feel your peace, and then my doubts start to go away. I have your protection, and you are my guide.

Yes, I am always here for you.

Reflections:

- Do you recognize that your doubts, distractions, and negative thoughts are ways Satan tries to separate you from God?
- Reread verse 2 Corinthians 10:5 and *"take captive every thought"* that is pulling you away from God.
- How can you get back on the path He created for you?

Humble and High Position

"The brother, in humble circumstances, ought to take pride in his high position" (James 1:9, NIV).

"Humble circumstances" sounds like being poor financially. If so, Lord, that's me.

Yes, but in comparison to others, you're not poor.

I know, but I feel like it. Throughout my life, I've always had to budget to save money. I don't have to be rich, Lord. I just don't want to worry about paying the bills.

Well, then watch how much you buy. You don't need anything. You spend money on what you want, not always what you need.

I know you're right. Forgive me, Lord. I shouldn't complain. I have enough if I keep it within my budget. I know you provide enough to meet my needs.

Yes, but I'm not talking about money. Why is the one in humble circumstances in a high position?

I don't know. It doesn't sound logical.

The person in humble circumstances isn't concerned with worldly possessions. That person may have them or may not. It doesn't matter because the person doesn't yearn for more money or things. The person is content.

I see. You're looking at my attitude.

I *view* the person in *humble circumstances* as one in a *high position*. I *cherish* that person who has a humble attitude and yearns to be with me. That person enjoys talking and listening to me. Unlike the self-sufficient person, who feels they don't need me or want to seek me. That's why that humble child of mine is above the self-sufficient person.

Yes, that's true, Lord. I never thought I'd say this, but I don't want a lot of money because it will cause me to take my eyes off of you, Lord. Please transform me so that I don't yearn for more money but instead yearn for you.

I'm proud of you because that's the first step. I know finances are always a struggle, but I have always provided for your needs. Continue to trust me.

Yes, Lord. You have a plan, and I will trust you. I will relax with you and not worry about the future. Help me to be responsible with my finances. Thank you, Lord, that you bring me true happiness and not the accumulation of things.

I'm slowly understanding...I should strive to have a humble attitude and yearn to be close to you because that's what you cherish and consider to be a high position.

Yes, my child.

Reflections:

- How are you like the brother in humble circumstances? How's your attitude?
- What are you yearning for?

Temptations: Dragged Away and Enticed

"When tempted, no one should say, 'God is tempting me.' For God cannot be tempted by evil, nor does he tempt anyone; but each one is tempted when, by his own evil desire, he is dragged away and enticed" (James 1:13-14, NIV).

Yup. You don't tempt me, Lord. Although, to be honest, the temptation is caused by me. Like it says, *"...each one is tempted when by his own evil desire."*

I'm the one in the struggle when that evil, outside force, comes upon me. It's offering me something I want or desire! I have a choice to give in to that temptation or not.

Yes, you have a choice. Temptations are different for everybody. For some, the attractions are for pleasure. For others, it is prestige and power. It doesn't matter what it is, but temptation has the same goal. Temptation benefits oneself. I'm glad you understand that temptation is your choice. Now I want you to reread the last phrase slowly.

"...he is dragged away and enticed."

What word(s) stand out to you?

"Dragged away" stands out. I was visualizing it as I was reading the verse.

"Dragging" means moving slowly, and "away" is like someone is pulling you. Some temptations seem innocent in the beginning, but they're slowly pushing you or pulling you away. For example, Satan

126

is dragging you away from following me. He wants you away from the support of your friends and family.

I know what you mean because mentally, I've moved away from others when I've been tempted before. I feel like I'm all alone in the dark.

When you're alone, you don't have support. As a result, it's easier for Satan to creep into your thoughts and whisper strong temptations into your ear. He wants to fill you with negativity and pull you down even further into *despair* so that you separate yourself from me and eventually turn your back on me.

Yes, when I feel alone, my mind gets negative and critical. During those times, it's so easy to imagine the worst. My mind keeps going on and on. It consumes me as I keep dwelling on all the negativity. I think about the worst of everything! I blow things out of proportion! How do I stop?

I want you to come to me and ask for protection from the temptation. Then when you call upon me, read my Word or devotion. Your negative thoughts won't just lessen; they will be replaced with my peace and wisdom. If you can, I want you to call a trusted Christian friend for support, too. I provide brothers and sisters in Christ to be my vessels to give you advice, guidance, and hugs.

Yes, Lord, I want that! Okay, when I feel negativity creeping in, I need to stop thinking, and go to you, and ask for protection from the enemy. Satan wants to pull me down, but you are mightier than he is. But what if I can't go to you? Sometimes I feel so pathetic and unworthy that I don't have the strength to get up and go to you. I feel like I'm just sitting in a hole of despair, and I can't move.

I know. With tears in my eyes, I see your despair and pain. Just stay there, but call out my name, and I will come to you. As I sit beside you, I will help you breathe slowly to gain some strength. I will tell you what to do next because I'm always here for you.

Yes, sitting with you always gives me peace and calms me down. Thank you for providing protection, erasing those negative thoughts in my mind, and replacing them with your love.

Reflections:

- How are you being tempted in your life? What is taking you away from spending time with God?
- What Christian friend can you seek out for support while you're faced with this temptation?

Trials and Temptations

"Don't be deceived, my dear brothers and sisters. Every good and perfect gift is from above, coming down from the Father of the heavenly lights, who does not change like shifting shadows. He chose to give us birth through the word of truth, that we might be a kind of firstfruits of all he created" (James 1:16-18, NIV).

You've been reading James 1 verse by verse. Now I want you to look over Chapter 1. What is the topic of this chapter so far?

This chapter is about trials and temptations.

I'm glad you understand the main topic. Now, as you reread verses 16-18, what stands out to you? Keep in mind that I'm discussing trials and temptations.

Since the passage is about trials and temptations, I see *"...Every good and perfect gift is from above..."* This supports the previous verses that you don't cause temptations because those are not good gifts. Satan is the one who tempts me to sin by enticing me with my evil desires. Sometimes I chose to give in to those temptations.

That's right. Sometimes I hear people say that I'm tempting them, but that's not true. Now listen carefully. Trials are when bad things in life happen to you. But your response to the trial can lead to temptations.

You're right. I'm the one choosing to give in to the temptations that Satan dangles in front of me.

I want you to learn something about temptations. When an unexpected situation arises, and it's taking a toll on you and your body,

you're in a weakened state. Satan sees this, so it's easier for him to tempt you and pull you away from me. He wants you to get angry, depressed, and pity yourself. He wants you to go down the hole of despair! Remember your first pregnancy?

Yes, Lord, that was the most challenging time in my life. I lost twenty pounds in one week and then another ten pounds a few weeks later. I was in constant pain for seven months! I felt like I had the stomach flu all day and all night! The vomiting wouldn't stop. I was always rushing to the bathroom. I would sit by the toilet and cry!

Remember what you asked me to do? What was my response?

I asked you to heal me! And you said, "My grace is sufficient!" So, I cried for you to take me to heaven because I couldn't bear the constant pain!

Your body was frail, fragile, and so was your mind. Satan knew that, so that's when he started to slip in negative thoughts about how dying would be more bearable.

I started thinking about how things could worsen, the "what ifs" started taking control of my mind. My thoughts were bringing me down into a hole of despair.

Yes, Satan was tempting you. You were giving in to his temptations of despair and anguish as you were dwelling on your negative thoughts. They were pulling you away from seeking me, but you had a choice. You could have given in to the temptations, or you could have sought me. You started to cry out to me. I knew you were in a deep hole and so weak, so what did I do?

In a loud voice in my mind, you yelled at me, "Stop it! Stop thinking about those negative thoughts!" You got my attention, so I stopped focusing on myself.

Yes, my voice was loud because your negative thoughts were blaring in your mind. But then I quietly and gently reminded you that I see and know everything you're going through. You needed to trust me. I told you that I would help you get through this and never leave you. Like I said before, my grace is sufficient.

Back then, I didn't understand how your grace was going to be sufficient for me. I thought healing me was the answer. You said your grace or love would help me through this difficult time.

Do you remember what I said? I told you I would sit by your side, talk to you, and ease you into sleep because that's when you didn't feel the pain.

Oh, yes, Lord! I remember those precious moments together. Your presence was mighty, powerful, yet gentle and loving. You caressed me in your strong and loving arms as I would fall asleep. The peace you gave me touched my heart and soul. That time in my life was so difficult, but I would go through it all again because I gained knowledge from being with you and feeling your Almighty presence! That's when my walk with you deepened more, and I finally understood how your grace was sufficient for me during that time!

You went through that trial, and your faith became stronger. There was a strength there that wasn't there before. But you gained this strength because you *didn't give in* to the temptation that Satan was dangling before you. You started to give into them, but you stopped. Instead, you cried out to me. It was your choice to come to me instead of giving in to those temptations.

Thank you, Lord, for stopping my negative thoughts and reassuring me of your love. You are with me as I walk through the deep valleys in my life. You have always been with me in my darkest hour.

I'm always here for you. Remember, your trials can weaken you, making you more susceptible to temptations, which lead you away

from me. Be aware of how you respond to the trials and don't give in to Satan's temptations.

I only give you good and perfect gifts.

Reflections:

- Think of a trial you've experienced. Then recall that specific time when you felt you were being tempted. What helped you resist falling into temptation?
- If you haven't been through this type of trial, be thankful. But remember and be aware that Satan is waiting to sneak in and pull you down into despair.

Take Note of This

"My dear brothers and sisters, take note of this: Everyone should be quick to listen, slow to speak and slow to become angry, because human anger does not produce the righteousness that God desires. Therefore, get rid of all moral filth and the evil that is so prevalent and humbly accept the word planted in you, which can save you" (James 1:19-21, NIV).

You've been reading verse by verse, but now I want you to read by paragraphs.

Let's look at the beginning of this paragraph. What do you see? What are you underlining?

"...take note of this: Everyone should be quick to listen, slow to speak, and slow to become angry." The words *"Take note of this"* mean it's very important, right?

Yes, I'm glad you noticed that.

Why doesn't it focus on faith, hope, and love? I thought those were the most important things to follow as a Christian?

Yes, you're right; faith, hope, and love are essential. However, when you think about it, those words are a bit vague to you. You need more concrete examples to understand them better so you can apply them to your life. If you follow the instructions above, you'll be showing faith, hope, and love.

You know me so well, Lord. I'm a simple person, and I want things to be easy to follow and understand.

What I want you to learn is *"...quick to listen, slow to speak and slow to become angry."*

I know I need to listen more and not speak too much. But I don't like the part *"slow to become angry"* because that is one of my weaknesses.

I know you think that, but it says *"slow to become angry."* **It doesn't say don't be angry.**

That's right, it doesn't! Hurray, so it's okay to get angry sometimes.

There are different types of anger. I don't want you exhibiting the selfish type of anger. However, there's the helping type of anger that's acceptable because you're helping others follow me. Remember, Jesus got upset when he saw that the temple was becoming a den of thieves? They were selling things for profit instead of having reverence for the temple of God.

I've always loved that part because it shows that Jesus wasn't a doormat or pushover. He was bold and strong! You've taught me how to use my anger and turn it into strength, boldness, and perseverance. I've needed those traits in my life.

Yes, I'm pleased when you have used your boldness to speak the truth and tell others about me. But let's go back to the beginning of verse 19, *"...be quick to listen, slow to speak, and slow to become angry."*

When you genuinely listen to the other person, you're open to hearing what that person is saying. You will be slow to speak because you're taking time to process what was said. Then you'll be slow to anger because you'll see things from the other person's perspective.

Usually, when people say they're listening, they're not. Many times, they're thinking about what they're going to say next to the person.

They're focusing on their thoughts or opinions instead of listening attentively.

That's true. So, I should genuinely listen, think about what the person is saying, and then respond. If I'm an attentive listener, I probably won't get angry because I understand the entire situation. You're so smart, Lord! Thank you for giving me concrete examples to help me be your vessel of love.

I'm pleased you're learning how to show my love to others. Now let's continue to verse 20, "*...for man's anger does not bring about the righteous life that God desires.*"

When you're angry, you can't experience the abundant, righteous life I want for you!

Yeah, I'm the one that stops me from experiencing your extraordinary and abundant life that you have for me. I realize that most of my angry moments are because of my selfishness and wanting my way! I know that's not the life you want for me. That's why the next word is, "*Therefore...*" You're emphasizing it because it's important. You're saying, "DO THIS!"

Yes, so let's continue to look at verse 21: "*Therefore, get rid of all moral filth and the evil that is so prevalent and humbly accept the word planted in you, which can save you.*"

You want me to rid myself of all moral filth and evil.

Yes, it's different for everyone, but for you, it's looking at your selfishness, control issues, and financial issues.

I know, Lord. Lately, you've been making me more aware of these issues and helping me with them. I never thought my financial issues would ever go away or lessen. I've always felt poor and had to budget my entire adult life. But you're changing my attitude toward money. I've always looked for ways to make some money on the side to help pay for expenses. It was constantly on my mind. But because of you, that desire is lessening! I'm finally trusting you to provide. I don't desire to have more. You are showing me that touching peoples' lives is more important than money. I want everyone to know you and love you, Lord! It's okay for me to continue to budget, but my focus is slowly changing. I'm amazed at how you can change my attitude! Thank you, Lord!

I know you've been struggling with this for a long time. I'm pleased that you're opening your heart, lessening your grip on money, and trusting me to provide for your needs. For others, moral filth and evil are prevalent in their lives! They need to get rid of it!

I understand, but that's so difficult for people to do. How can they rid themselves of moral filth and evil?

They need to *"...humbly accept the word planted in you, which can save you."* **They need to have a humble heart and ask me to forgive them for their sins. Then accept Jesus as their Savior and welcome him into their life. Jesus is the** *"word planted in you."* **After Jesus comes into their life, they start having a relationship with me as they get to know me more and more. I created you to have a relationship with me.**

Here's an analogy...The light bulb was created to give light and use the source of electricity to fulfill that purpose. It can't use the power of gasoline to fulfill its purpose because it wasn't made that way. I know this is hard to understand, but I created you for a specific purpose too. You can only use my power to fulfill that purpose. There is no other power source. Many people try to have a fulfilling life without me. But in the end, their life isn't satisfied because they didn't fulfill the specific purpose I created them for.

I'm slowly grasping your concept that I am created for a specific purpose. You want me to do certain things but do them with the power you give me. I'm still learning this because I tend to follow my way instead of your way. I know it's hard for people to believe in you and follow you because they want to control their own life. They want their way. However, you know what's best for their life because you created them. You know what will truly satisfy them. I never thought that having you in my life would give me inner peace and joy, especially when there's a mess around me. You are wonderful, Lord! My prayer is that everyone gets to know you and loves you, God.

Reflections:

- How are you doing with "...*should be quick to listen, slow to speak and slow to become angry...*"?
- What "*moral filth and evil*" does God want you to get rid of?
- Is your life fulfilling because of what you're doing or what God is doing with you?

One-Way Apology

Hey God,

You said to write about this time in my life because it's an important lesson I learned, but I sit here a little hesitant. Why?

You're hesitating because it was a time that you were very *hurt* by someone. It was a painful time, even though you learned a lot. Nobody likes revisiting a hurtful time. But I want you to write about this because everyone needs to learn this lesson.

Okay, please help me as I try to recall what happened.

(I was attending church, and a new pastor was in charge. After a while, the pastor's wife came up to me. I felt she was yelling at me, but she probably wasn't. She commented: "You're just like the previous pastor. You're always talking to people, and they're talking to you. Who do you think you are? People are continually going to you for things. You're in charge of a lot of activities! Why do you have to do everything?" She said other hurtful things, but I don't remember. I guess that's good. I didn't say anything because I was so shocked by her words! I was thinking... You're mad at me because people like me and because I'm active and helping in the church? I couldn't believe it! So, I walked away. If I stayed, my temper would rage at this pitiful lady. I remember the conversation we had, Lord, after she talked to me.)

Lord, can you believe what she said to me? She's crazy! She's mad at me for my strengths and for helping the church! Nobody has ever yelled at me for this!

She is jealous of the previous pastor. People adored him because he's so loving. They flocked to him for advice. She's always been

envious of the previous pastor. So, when she met you and saw all the things you do at church, you reminded her of him. So, she took out her anger on you.

I know I'm similar to the previous pastor. But what that lady said was hurtful and horrible!

I know this is hard to understand, but let me handle her. Right now, my concern is what's happening to you.

That's right. I didn't do anything wrong! What's the matter with her? She makes me so mad! And she calls herself a pastor's wife! Ugh! I want to tell other people, but I know I can't. I understand that this is her problem and not mine, but I'm still so mad at her for saying those awful, hurtful things to me. I feel helpless because I want justice, and I can't say anything. I want her to pay for what she said to me! Aaahhh, Lord!

I know. I see your pain and hurt. You're right about not saying anything. If you did, it would cause a big scandal and division in the church.

(Lord, as the days went by, every time I saw her, I was outwardly cordial, but inside I was furious. A good friend told me how lovely the pastor's wife was to her and what she did for her. I held my tongue, but inside I was boiling mad! My thoughts were becoming negative and ugly toward her. I kept thinking, "Someone needs to shut her up and tell her the truth!")

I know that all of this is unfair, and you want to yell at her, but you can't.

Ugh! Lord, then what can I do?

I want you to apologize and forgive her.

What? Are you crazy, Lord? She's the one that needs to apologize to me and ask me for forgiveness! NOT ME!

I know you're upset, and I understand how you feel. I know what the pastor's wife did was wrong. But right now, I'm concerned about *you*, your attitude, and especially your negative thoughts toward her. Look what's happening to you. You're turning into her.

What? I'm not like her!

Would you agree that she puts down others and thinks she's higher or better than others?

Yes! She's terrible!

Well, that's what you've been doing too. The only difference is instead of saying the words, you're thinking about them in your head. She voices them out loud, but you're thinking them. Remember, that's a sin too. Sin is a sin to me.

Oh my gosh, Lord! Yuck! I don't like this, but I get it. I'm sorry. Forgive me for my wrongful thoughts and especially my negative attitude. These past few weeks have made me very critical of her. Now that I think about it, her negativity has crept into my heart and invaded other parts of my life! I'm becoming critical and short with others too. Yuck! Lord, help me get rid of all of this!

I will help you get rid of these awful thoughts and attitudes. But, first, I want you to apologize and forgive her.

How can I do that, Lord? I can't talk to her. When I look at her, I despise her.

I understand, and I will help you. Listen carefully to my instructions. I want you to tell her: *"Because of what you said to me, I have become negative and critical. God doesn't like my attitude and what I'm becoming. I apologize for my negativity and critical spirit towards you. So, I'm asking you to forgive me."*

Say these words and nothing else. Look straight at her when you say them and count to three when you're done speaking. Slowly turn around and walk away. *Do not* **turn around and look at her. Keep walking away!**

What? Oh, man, Lord. That's going to be hard. But okay, Lord, I'll say those words, even though your instructions are strange. You need to be right next to me because I don't know if I can do this.

I will be there with you. I'm always with you.

(So, I apologized to her and asked her for forgiveness with the words God gave me. God said to count to three before turning around, so I counted. When I turned around and started to walk away, God said…)

Keep walking. Don't turn around. You did your part. Your heart is clean before me. That's all that matters now.

(As I was walking away, she started yelling at me again! I couldn't believe it! I had just apologized to her, and she was yelling at me!)

Lord, now I understand your unusual directions about keep walking and not turning around to face her. I didn't expect her to yell at me!

I wanted you to count to three because it would have been odd if you apologized and abruptly turned around. By facing her and staying there for three seconds, your words were genuine and honest. If you had walked away quickly, she would have thought that you didn't mean it. If you had turned and looked back at her while she was yelling at you, you would have taken the apology back, and forgiveness would not have happened.

That's so true, Lord! You're so smart! I'm so glad I followed your strange and specific directions.

Yes, I'm pleased you did too. So, did I help you get rid of your awful thoughts and attitude?

Yes, you did, Lord! Thank you for being by my side. I didn't think you could wipe away all those negative feelings and anger inside of me. But because I was hurting and being pulled down, I needed to do something. I'm so glad I listened to you! Now I feel cleansed, and the burden of a critical spirit is gone. I don't hate her anymore. I didn't think that was possible. Thank you, Lord!

(Years later, I saw her at a church gathering. She greeted my other sisters with hugs, but not me. I expected that, and to my surprise, I wasn't hurt. Later on, that night, God said to praise her for creating the slideshow for the church. Without the Lord's love, I wouldn't have been able to do that. After I complimented her for what she made, she didn't say anything nice to me in return. I was hoping she would, but she didn't, and again, I wasn't bothered. I smiled and thanked the Lord for how He cleansed me of that hurtful event a long time ago. He had truly restored me because I could honestly say that I wasn't bothered or hurt by her anymore. This incident in my life has taught me that sometimes I need to give a one-way apology. That's the phrase God gave me to describe that time in my life. Usually, when a person apologizes, the other person does too. You both feel reconciled and better.)

I know this was a difficult situation, but there will be times in your life when you need to make peace with me and give a one-way apology. It's hard to do, but your soul and spirit will always be at peace when you do. Remember, I want you to be clean before me. So, don't worry about the other person.

Thank you, Lord, for teaching me this powerful lesson. I've never heard a sermon on a one-way apology until now, Lord. Thank you. You are amazing! You can do the impossible!

Reflections:

- Has someone hurt you? Is God telling you to give a "one-way apology" and to forgive that person?
- Even if the person isn't in your life anymore, you can still give a "one-way apology." God wants you to be clean before him and get rid of those awful thoughts and attitudes. You could write a letter to that person, even if they have passed away because writing it down makes the apology real to you. Or perhaps you can visualize the person in front of you and then give your "one-way apology." The important thing is saying your apology to free yourself of past hurts and be clean before the Lord.

Critical Thoughts

"If you really keep the royal law found in Scripture, 'Love your neighbor as yourself,' you are doing right. But if you show favoritism, you sin and are convicted by the law as law-breakers. For whoever keeps the whole law and yet stumbles at just one point is guilty of breaking all of it. For he who said, 'You shall not commit adultery,' also said, 'You shall not murder.' If you do not commit adultery but do commit murder, you have become a law-breaker." (James 2:8-11, NIV).

What stands out to you?

I sense you want me to focus on favoritism, but I'm not sure why. I have always tried not to show favoritism to people I meet and treat everyone the same.

You're right. I want you to focus on this because you *are* showing favoritism without knowing it.

Huh? How?

You don't like the homeless, the ones taking drugs and refusing to go to the shelters. That is favoritism because you don't mind helping some of the homeless, but not all of them. When you prefer one group of people over another, and you're looking down upon the other group, that is favoritism.

That's true, God. I am looking down upon those that refuse to go to the shelters. It's easier to help the ones that are trying to help themselves. I've met people who were homeless and struggling financially. They were doing their best to remedy their situation. I had compassion toward them and tried to help them. However, since the media shows some homeless people that drink, take drugs, and refuse to go to the shelters, I've been critical of them. I don't understand why they're refusing to get the help the state is offering.

You don't understand because you don't know their situation. You don't know how or why those people became homeless. Since you don't know, you shouldn't condemn or judge them. I'm the only judge.

You're right, Lord. Forgive me for my attitude towards them. I don't know the entire situation, so I have no right to judge or look down upon them.

Yes, the homeless are my children too. Unfortunately, you don't know all the facts about each one.

I'm sorry, Lord, forgive me. Thank you for making me aware of favoritism in my life. My attitude is so arrogant! I'm so embarrassed, Lord. Forgive me of my critical spirit. Help me love my neighbor.

I'm not just talking about the homeless. You show favoritism or have a critical spirit toward people different from you because they don't think as you do. I know you don't believe you're righteous, but sometimes you think you're better than others because you try to follow my standards of goodness. So, when others don't agree with you or live differently from you, you look down upon them. Even though it's subtle and you don't say anything to their faces, those critical thoughts are in your head. I see that little arrogance in you. You're putting them down silently in your mind. I see it even if they don't. It's still an ugly sin to me.

Oh man, Lord, forgive me for my critical spirit. You're right! Sin is a sin to you. One sin is not worse than another. My subtle arrogance is still a sin. How do I stop this righteous attitude?

When thoughts coming from a righteous attitude enter your head, stop and ask me for wisdom. I'll remind you that I have made every person different. People that are different from you can share the gospel with people you can't reach. I know you want everyone to know and love me. When you were younger, you told me that you're not cultured and poised, but rather the opposite.

Yes, I remember that conversation.

Then I told you that it is okay to be different because I made you that way. The cultured and poised woman will be able to share the gospel with another refined woman. While you will continue to tell others about me in the way I created you to. Others have told you they like your openness and honesty. They've said it's refreshing! So, continue to be you and share with your loud love.

"Loud love." I like that Lord. Yup, that's me! My friends have told me I'm very animated and expressive, so I guess that's loud love!

Remember, when you don't understand people or why they act a certain way, remember I created them that way. I have a purpose for everyone.

Yes, Lord, please forgive me. When these subtle, critical thoughts creep into my head, I will remember that you made them that way, and you love them!

I know you also feel judged by others too, and that they look down upon you. Remember, I made you like this! Don't ever feel you're inferior to others. I want you to forgive those people that look down upon you because you do the same thing too.

You're right. Help me be more aware of my subtle, critical thoughts towards others. Please fill me with your unconditional love. Thank you for opening my eyes.

Reflections:

- Are there people in your life that you look down upon or think you're better than?
- Think of those closest to you. Do you ever have critical or judgmental thoughts towards them?
- How is God asking you to change those thoughts?

Wise and Understanding

"Who is wise and understanding among you? Let them show it by their good life, by deeds done in the humility that comes from wisdom" (James 3:13, NIV).

What do you see that you didn't see before or remember?

I remember the word "wise" but not the "understanding" part. If you're wise, you're probably understanding and compassionate too, huh?

Yes, but let's looks at the word "understanding" again. What does an understanding person look like? It's like that phrase you use with the younger children when you teach Sunday school. Do you remember it?

Do you mean the phrase I used with hand motions? 'Stop, Look, Listen, Shhh!"

> Stop (with both hands up in front of them),
> Look (both hands cupped near their eyes),
> Listen (both hands cupped by their ears),
> Shhh! (pointer finger in front of their mouth).

Yes, that's the phrase and motions I'm referring to. You taught them to calm them down, get their attention, and focus on the lesson ahead. I want to add another step to that phrase to learn what an understanding person is like. Here's my version:

"Stop, Look, Step back, Listen, Shhh."

Why did you add "step back"?

When you step back, you pause and take yourself out of the picture or situation. It helps calm you down, so you can earnestly listen to the person instead of thinking of what to say next. It's not necessary to share your thoughts at this time. I want you to see, feel, and understand the other person's perspective. Yet many people respond quickly; that's why their words are full of anger and very hurtful. Instead, I want you to gather your thoughts together and ask me for wisdom. Then you're able to share your opinion with the other person.

Let's look at the phrase again with hand motions, but with my suggestions that follow.

"Stop" with hands up in front;
> *you're surrendering yourself to that person*

"Look" with hands by your eyes;
> *you're focusing on that person*

"Step back" by taking a physical step backward;
> *you're stepping out of the situation so your feelings won't cloud your judgment*

"Listen" with hands by your ears;
> *you're listening attentively and blocking out distractions*

"Shhh!" with a finger by your mouth;
> *you're not going to speak, but be quiet and listen with your heart*

Wow, Lord, that's cool how you enriched my simple phrase. So now, this phrase is for everyone to learn and practice. I won't look upon it as a tool for only children, but a tool for me to practice true understanding when I'm with people.

Now let's look at the latter part of the verse, *"...Let them show it by their good life, by deeds done in the humility that comes from wisdom."*

As you gain wisdom from me, you become humble, then you naturally serve others and follow me. It gets easier. Wisdom is shown by what you do with a humble heart.

So, as I keep seeking or asking you for wisdom, I will become humble. I like it when you said, "naturally serve others." This gives me comfort to know serving others won't be a struggle as it is now. Thank you, Lord, for giving me hope that things will get better! Help me remember your revised version of...Stop...Look...Step Back...Listen...Shhh!

Reflections:

- What part of the phrase "Stop, Look, Step back, Listen, Shhh!" do you need to work on?
- How is wisdom being shown by what you do with a humble heart?

Envy and Selfish Ambition

"But if you harbor bitter envy and selfish ambition in your hearts, do not boast about it or deny the truth. Such 'wisdom' does not come down from heaven but is earthly, unspiritual, demonic. For where you have envy and selfish ambition, there you find disorder and every evil practice" (James 3:14-16, NIV).

How or why would anyone consider "bitter envy and selfish ambition" wisdom?

It's wisdom to them because they're using strategies and planning on getting ahead and making more money. They think that's an intelligent plan. So to them, it's wisdom!

Oh, never thought of it that way. Now I understand how some people would consider that wisdom.

No, that's you too.

Huh?

You don't have bitter envy, but sometimes you have selfish ambition because you want your way at your job. You want people to follow you.

Oh, I see. I don't view it as selfish ambition, but it is selfish. Yes, I want my way because I think my plan or strategies are better for the company and customers. Wow, Lord, you're opening my eyes!

So, don't boast or deny the truth about what you're doing. Instead, you need to be honest and face the fact that what you're doing is wrong.

So that's why I need to seek your wisdom and ask you how to handle situations?

Yes. You sought my wisdom at work. I know it was hard, but you obeyed me, and you received many injustices for doing it. I was proud of you because it caused you heartache.

It was difficult, but I remember having peace because I knew I was following you.

Look at the last verse, "... *where you have envy and selfish ambition, there you find disorder and every evil practice.*"

I understand the disorder. When things are like that, you can't trust anyone, especially your boss or coworkers, because everyone thinks about themselves. And "...*every evil practice...*" brings out the worse in people.

Yes. Selfish ambition causes people to do unexpected things they didn't think they were capable of doing. So, when you want your way or trying to solve a problem, first ask me for wisdom. Then I'll tell you what to do.

Okay, Lord. But sometimes, I don't see how I'm being selfish, so please make me aware of my selfishness, then I will come to you.

Just keep talking with me. I'll tell you.

Thank you, Lord.

Reflections:

- When did you harbor bitter envy or had selfish ambition? How would things be different if you had asked God for wisdom?

(If you want to read about what happened at work, read the devotion "Step In My Steps.")

The Wisdom That Comes from Heaven

"But the wisdom that comes from heaven is first of all pure; then peace-loving, considerate, submissive, full of mercy and good fruit, impartial and sincere" (James 3:17, NIV).

Look at the beginning words again: *"...wisdom that comes from heaven."* This is the wisdom I want you to seek and have. You're always asking me for wisdom. So, let's slowly go through each adjective.

You're right. I want your wisdom.

***"Pure"* wisdom is perfect and filled with love for you. I only want what's best for you!**

Thank you, Lord, that your wisdom is perfect. You know what I need and what I should do to have a full and abundant life with you.

Yes, you're my precious child that I love so much.

Help me to have "pure wisdom" toward others too.

Keep abiding with me, and you will gain heaven's "pure wisdom."

***Peace-loving* wisdom seeks out what is best for everyone. With my "peace-loving" wisdom, you will see unity, where everyone is working together.**

I understand what you mean. Instead of reacting, I need to be calm and pause to evaluate what's best for everyone. Then I can hear your wisdom. When I see my coworkers or my family working together, it brings me such JOY! I love unity!

Peace-loving wisdom is also keeping the peace for now, instead of solving the problem. So sometimes you need to wait and trust me.

I understand, but I want to help solve the problem. So, I need to seek your wisdom first.

Considerate wisdom is thinking about others before you and what is best for them. Of course, you understand this concept, but you usually think about yourself first.

I know, I'm so selfish! I want your love to flow through me to other people instead of thinking of myself. Please shout to me instead of whispering. Keep bugging me until I obey you. Like yesterday, you told me to give some money to someone, but I didn't. I couldn't stop thinking about it. So now you're bugging me again, thank you! So, I will set the money aside and give it to her. Until I do this, I know my heart will be unsettled.

I know it's hard, but I'm proud of you because eventually, you obey me.

Submissive wisdom is submitting to me, following me, and trusting me when you're unsure of submitting to authority. I will place people in power over you that you will question. So, you must seek me and trust me for answers. Then I will tell you what to do.

It's hard for me to be submissive to people. I don't trust anyone entirely because everyone makes mistakes. I have a hard time complying with authority when I know what they're doing is wrong and hurtful.

I know it's difficult, but when you've sought me for answers in the past, I was by your side. You were able to submit to earthly authority even though you thought what they were doing was wrong.

When?

Your manager did some wrong things at your company, which was brought to the boss's attention. The boss was aware that the manager was terrible but supported the manager's bad decision. You came to me in tears. I told you I know what happened is unacceptable, but you have to let go of your anger, accept the results, and move on. However, moving on doesn't mean you agree with the decision. It is an act of submission to your superior. I told you to trust me because complying with the authority will open the manager's eyes and see how Christians act. In the long run, that is more important.

Yes, I remember that incident. You're right. You were by my side and gave me wisdom and guidance. It was hard for me to keep quiet, but I did. After a while, the manager came to me, asking for help. I was shocked by what she said: "I know the way you reacted to everything is because you're a Christian. I would like your advice on helping the other employees, so they can accept this situation the way you are and move on." Lord, you gave me your wisdom that I shared with her so she could help the others. She accepted your words of wisdom that resulted in happier employees that could move on.

I know it's difficult to be submissive. Still, I will take care of everything when you're submissive to me and trust me. Remember Romans 8:28 (KJV) *"And we know that all things work together for good to them that love God, to them who are called according to His purpose."*

Full of mercy **wisdom is forgiving others when they don't deserve it. I understand forgiveness is hard, so ask me to help you forgive people. This will take time, but as you continue reading my word and praying, I will guide you and help you forgive others.**

You are powerful, Lord, because you have helped me forgive others. Only with you by my side was I able to forgive that person. It took me time to forgive him because I was hurt by what he said. He asked me to forgive him. I was honest and told him I couldn't at the moment, but I eventually would because the Lord would help me. I think it was about three years later when I saw him at a friend's funeral. I went up to him, told him I forgave him about 2 years ago, and hugged him. He smiled and said, "Thank you." Thank you, Lord, for helping me forgive him.

Yes, I'm glad you forgave him. When you did, your heart was set free. It was like a burden was lifted off of you. You had peace in your heart again.

Yes!

***Good fruit* wisdom is when you follow me and become my vessel to spread my love to others. When they are touched by my love through you, you are showing good fruit. Christians begin growing and showing good fruit when they first accept Jesus as their Savior. They continue to produce good fruit as they learn to follow me and obey me. Then as their faith in me matures, there's more good fruit.**

It's a privilege when you choose me to be a vessel for you. It brings me joy! I always feel I'm blessed more than the person I helped. My heart is overflowing with gratitude to you.

Yes, my child, I'm pleased when you're being my vessel and spreading my love!

***Impartial* wisdom means being open and able to look at both sides. Unfortunately, people tend to forget about *being open* because that is the hardest part. Being open means to be willing to change one's mind and admitting that they are wrong.**

That's true. I've seen people act as mediators in their situations and look at both sides to understand the problem. However, it's difficult for some to be open and realize that they are wrong. I've seen people blame the other person instead of admitting their fault. Sometimes that person makes an excuse instead of accepting their wrongdoing.

Yes, I've seen this happen many times. That's why it's essential to be open, listen to the other person, and don't let your pride get in the way. You've taught your children this by example. Remember, your daughter told you she doesn't know many adults that will listen to young people and apologize to them? She said you would listen, be open to change your mind, and admit you were wrong. Then you would apologize to her.

Yes, Lord. Thank you for reminding me. My children have said that apologizing is an admirable trait they want to emulate. I was shocked because I didn't know I was teaching them this valuable lesson. I would just apologize because I was wrong. This is because of you, Lord, and not me. You were the one that would tell me to apologize.

Impartial wisdom knows the facts of the situation, setting aside one's opinion when looking at both sides. Remember what your dad taught you?

Yes. When I was little, I was angry at someone. I remember yelling. Then my dad sat me down in his bedroom and said, "Before you get angry, you must learn about all the facts." Then he started to reveal some facts I wasn't aware of. When I learned about them, my heart softened, and I wasn't angry anymore. He told me that you won't be mad when you know more about the facts or situation. Instead, you'll be understanding. He was right. I love him! He's so wise!

Yes, I love your dad too. He's a remarkable man of God! He has a *heart of gold!* Everywhere he goes, he touches people's lives with my love.

Yes, I love him so much, Lord! He has taught me so much about life. I thank you and praise you for blessing me with a wonderful dad!

Sincere wisdom is simple to understand because you've learned it from listening and watching your parents. Sincere wisdom is when someone genuinely loves you. That person will give you insight, or truth, even though it may hurt you.

Yes, Lord, you're right. My parents will tell the truth because they love me, my family, and all the people they meet. Their sincere wisdom is something I've always felt in my heart and seen in their lives.

Wow, Lord. This was long, but thank you for explaining *the wisdom from heaven* in more detail and giving me examples! Since I'm always asking you for wisdom, now I have something to reread and follow. Thank you, Lord! You know I needed this! You know me so well!

Pure wisdom is perfect and filled with love for you. I only want what's best for you!

Peace-loving wisdom seeks out what is best for everyone. It's also keeping the peace for now instead of trying to solve the problem. Sometimes you need to wait and trust me.

Considerate wisdom is thinking about others before you.

Submissive wisdom is submitting to me, following me, and trusting me when you question the authority that is placed over you. I will tell you what to do.

Full of mercy wisdom is forgiving others when they don't deserve it.

Good fruit wisdom is when you follow me and become my vessel to spread my love to others.

Impartial wisdom knows the facts of the situation, sets aside one's opinion when looking at both sides.

Sincere wisdom is when someone genuinely loves you. That person will give you insight or truth, even though it may hurt you.

Reflections:

- Eight adjectives describe God's wisdom. Select one and apply it to your life today.
- Tomorrow or next week, select another one and apply that to your life.
- How can you seek his wisdom in every decision and circumstance?

A Friend of God or the World?

"What causes fights and quarrels among you? Don't they come from your desires that battle within you? You desire but do not have, so you kill. You covet, but you cannot get what you want, so you quarrel and fight. You do not have because you do not ask God. When you ask, you do not receive, because you ask with wrong motives, that you may spend what you get on your pleasures. You adulterous people, don't you know that friendship with the world means enmity against God? Therefore, anyone who chooses to be a friend of the world becomes an enemy of God. Or do you think Scripture says without reason that he jealously longs for the spirit he has caused to dwell in us. But he gives us more grace. That is why Scripture says: 'God opposes the proud, but shows favor to the humble.' Submit yourselves, then, to God. Resist the devil, and he will flee from you. Come near to God, and he will come near to you. Wash your hands, you sinners, and purify your hearts, you double-minded. Grieve, mourn and wail. Change your laughter to mourning and your joy to gloom. Humble yourselves before the Lord, and he will lift you up" (James 4:1-10, NIV).

There are many essential gems for you here, so let's read them slowly. First, reread verses 1-3. What do you see?

My desires cause my fights and quarrels. I see my selfishness. When I was younger, I used to yell and get angry because I didn't get my way. Everyone told me I had a bad temper. As I got older, you taught me that my bad temper is my selfishness. You're right. My fights and quarrels stem from wanting my way. Yuck!

Yes, so stop and think; ask yourself why you're getting angry. Are you being selfish? I know it's difficult, but being aware of your selfishness is the first step towards maturity.

Then there are my "Gimme Prayers...Gimme this Lord, Gimme that Lord!" I'm asking you with the wrong motives. Oh Lord, help me!

Selfishness leads to selfish motives. But again, being aware of this is another beginning step. Now reread verses 4-6. What are they telling you?

They're telling me that when the world is more important to me than you, I'm hurting you. I'm being an enemy against you when I think about myself and want control of my destiny. I'm trying to be self-sufficient instead of depending on you. I'm sorry, Lord, for causing you pain! I don't want to be your enemy. You're waiting and longing for the Holy Spirit to thrive in me.

Yes, I patiently wait for you. My arms are open and always ready to welcome you back. My heart yearns and aches for you to listen to the Holy Spirit because He can comfort your soul and help you with your selfishness. I know you don't like it when your selfishness is blaring at you. However, when it does, you humble yourself and come to me.

Yup, it sucks when my selfishness overwhelms me. So, thank you for giving me grace and forgiving me. I'm sorry I keep messing up by choosing to be a friend of the world instead of depending on you.

I know. Continue rereading verses 7-10. Look at the *beginning* of verse 7, *"Submit yourselves, then, to God. Resist the devil, and he will flee from you."* What does this mean?

When I realize my sinfulness, I need to submit myself to you.

"Submit yourselves..." You want me to humble myself, go to you, and follow you. You want my attitude to be, "Your will, not my will."

When you say those words and mean them, you will trust me for your future. You'll stop worrying about things because I have a plan

for your life. You'll stop trying to control situations to prevent the "what if" scenarios. You'll be trusting me. Remember Romans 8:28, *"And we know that all things work together for good to them that love God, to them who are called according to His purpose"* (NIV).

Yeah, but I struggle submitting to you and wanting my way. It's a battle every day, Lord.

I know, but being aware of this struggle leads toward maturity. You can't fix the problem until you see what's going on. That's why awareness is so important. You struggle between what you want versus the plans I have for you. But here's some encouragement. There have been times when you have chosen to trust me. You have seen how things worked out perfectly because I'm by your side and guiding you!

Yes, Lord! You're right! But I'm a slow learner because I still struggle with wanting my will instead of following you.

I know, but don't be hard on yourself. I understand that this is an ongoing battle. Reread the latter part of verse 7.

Okay... *"Resist the devil, and he will flee from you."*

Resisting the devil is difficult because he's crafty and sneaky. First, you must realize that he is the author of distractions. It can be anything that takes you away from spending time with me. For example, you were just on your phone and looking into R95 masks since an ad popped up. But I told you to stop and read that later. If you had continued, you wouldn't be spending time with me now. So be aware of the subtle distractions.

Resisting the devil is also avoiding temptations. You know what's not good for you. Temptations are worse than distractions. They don't just stop you from spending time with me; they pull you *away from me*. It's difficult to walk away from temptations, so *avoid*

them! *Please don't go near them.* For some, it may mean taking websites off the computer or not walking into a bar, or turning the TV off, or not gossiping with friends. You know the temptations that pull you away from me. Avoid them! When you submit to me, stop the distractions, and avoid the temptations, the devil will flee! It's an ongoing battle between you and the enemy. You need to fight the enemy every day, every minute.

I get it. Every day is a battle. I need to do something to resist the devil. I can't just complain and grumble about the distractions and temptations. When I do, I get stuck and can't move forward with you. It's easier to keep dwelling on the negative things than submitting to you.

Yes, I won't force you because it's your choice. But look at what I said in verse 8.

It says, *"Come near to God, and he will come near to you. Wash your hands, you sinners, and purify your hearts, you double-minded."*

I know how difficult it is to *begin making the right choices*. As soon as you start coming near to me, I will *come near* you and help you. When you repent and wash your hands, I will purify your heart and take away the filth of your past and your double-minded ways. You thought you could live with the world's values and still follow me. But you can't because the world's values are in contradiction to mine. You need to acknowledge that and let go of the world's hold on you. I will help you fight it.

I'm sad to admit it, but there are times I have convinced myself that compromise is okay, but it's not in your eyes. Forgive me, Lord.

I forgive you every time you come to me. Now read the last two verses.

"Grieve, mourn and wail. Change your laughter to mourning and your joy to gloom. Humble yourselves before the Lord, and he will lift you up."
Huh? Change laughter to mourning? Why?

Many things that are happening in your life grieve and hurt the Holy Spirit. Ask the Holy Spirit to open your eyes to these things. He will show you so you can repent, weep, and mourn at how you're hurting him.

Would you please show me?

Sometimes you watch shows or comics that are somewhat distasteful with foul language. I know you don't laugh hysterically, but they make things and people seem funny at the expense of putting people down. I want you to avoid engaging in those types of things because they will influence your thinking.

I understand. You don't want me to fill my mind with foul language and unpleasant things. I need to purify my heart and humbly go to you.

Lord, reading these verses is hard. It's taking time to process everything because they make me confront my issues and be honest with myself. I need to evaluate my motives and my selfishness. It's difficult because I see ugliness and sin. I need to make a lot of changes. So, guide me and give me your wisdom. Only you can fill me with inner peace and joy! I don't want to grieve the Holy Spirit!

Yes, I know this is hard, but I'm always right beside you in this battle. Remember, I'm the conqueror and deliverer! So, equip yourself with my Scriptures, my words.

Reflections:

This battle between you and the enemy is a life-long process. So we need to focus on the hard questions.

- When are you a friend of God?
- When are you a friend of the world?
- To be specific, how can you flee from Satan's distractions and temptations?
- Be honest with yourself.
- Evaluate your motives.
- How is your selfishness affecting your decisions?
- Equip yourself with God's promises. Find a few verses to memorize to strengthen you.

Show My Compassion

"One day Peter and John were going up to the temple at the time of prayer—at three in the afternoon. Now a man who was lame from birth was being carried to the temple gate called Beautiful, where he was put every day to beg from those going into the temple courts. When he saw Peter and John about to enter, he asked them for money. Peter looked straight at him, as did John. Then Peter said, 'Look at us!' So, the man gave them his attention, expecting to get something from them. Then Peter said, 'Silver or gold I do not have, but what I do have I give you. In the name of Jesus Christ of Nazareth, walk.' Taking him by the right hand, he helped him up, and instantly the man's feet and ankles became strong. He jumped to his feet and began to walk. Then he went with them into the temple courts, walking and jumping, and praising God. When all the people saw him walking and praising God, they recognized him as the same man who used to sit begging at the temple gate called Beautiful, and they were filled with wonder and amazement at what had happened to him" (Acts 3:1-10, NIV).

Peter heals a crippled man. I don't remember the part where it says *"Peter looked straight at him"* then Peter said, *"Look at us!"* They wanted his full attention.

Sometimes you're like that disabled man when you're talking with me.

Yes, sometimes I'm distracted by thinking of other things. I'm sorry, Lord. There's a big difference when you have my full attention, huh?

Yes, please focus on me and forget the distractions of the world. I want you to look intently at me and come to my open arms of love and listen.

Now, look at what Peter does right after saying, *"In the name of Jesus Christ of Nazareth, walk."*

Verse 7 says, *"Taking him by the right hand, he helped him up..."*

What do you see Peter doing?

I see Peter squatting down and bending over to get the man's right hand. Then I see Peter put his other hand behind his back to help him up. So now they're both standing.

Peter didn't just heal him; he also helped him up! So I don't want you to only pray for people. Please help them physically, emotionally, financially in whatever way you can. By helping others in these ways, you're showing my compassion. So please touch their hearts and souls for me with actions and not just words.

Yes, Lord.

Reflections:

- Are you focusing on God or getting distracted by other things?
- How are you helping by praying for the people?
- What else can you do to help them physically, emotionally and financially?

The Best Advice from Mom

Share your mom's best advice for mothers. You're always telling others about her and what you learned from her. So, share this wisdom I gave to your mom.

You're right, Lord. When I was in high school, I was furious about something that had happened. I can't remember now, but I know I was upset! When I came home, I told my mom about the incident. She gave me milk and cookies or some snack. My mom listened to me vent for a long time! Finally, I felt better and went to my room.

Later on, that evening, while I was doing my homework, she asked me to talk about what happened at school. At first, I didn't know what she was referring to. She refreshed my memory. She started to give me some advice about how to handle the situation. I understood and thanked her.

Years later, Lord, you reminded me about this incident and the important lesson she taught me. You told me to never forget it!

Yes, I kept that critical incident in your heart to help you become a better mom and help others. Your mom is amazing! She demonstrated what a good mother is. Now let's review what happened. What did she do?

She listened to me vent!

This is the crucial part. What *didn't* your mom do?

Huh?

Your mom didn't do something when you were venting. This is the crucial part of the advice. Think!

She didn't scold or yell at me for my sassy attitude and temper!

YES! She sat there and listened to you attentively without interrupting you. She wanted to understand your feelings because you were upset and hurt. She allowed you to vent. You needed to do that!

Yup, my mom is a saint! She is so loving and patient, unlike me!

Then what did she do that night? Why did she do it later on?

That night, she came to me and gave me advice about how to handle the situation.

Years later, I asked her for clarification since you reminded me of this significant incident. Why did she give me advice *later that night* instead of telling me after hearing about the situation? She said she knew I wouldn't listen to her earlier because I was upset and hurt. So, scolding me wouldn't have helped me either.

Yes. Your mom is wise. Do you know why?

Yes. When I became a new mom, I told her I prayed to you, Lord, for wisdom because I was scared to be a mom. I knew all of my faults and didn't think I would be a good mom like her. She smiled and told me that she prayed for wisdom also—to be a good mom because her mom died when she was young. She still prays every day for her children and asks for wisdom.

So, my mom was probably praying as she was listening to me yell and vent, huh?

Yes, she was. I told her to talk to you later when you're calm and willing to listen to her advice.

Here's the *best advice* for mothers.
Truly listen to others when they are hurt or upset.
Don't think about what to say or give advice.
Instead, show that person you value them by
taking the time to listen attentively.
Later on, you can talk more and discuss some possible solutions.

Who wants to talk to someone that will immediately scold them for their bad behavior? This advice isn't just for a parent and a child. This is how we should treat *all* of our relationships!

Thank you for blessing me with a patient mom that loves you and seeks your wisdom! She shows your love by example and isn't even aware of it. Her love flows naturally. She's the best humble servant I know!

I'm not patient like my mom, but I wanted to follow her example. So, I told my four children about this incident. I explained that I'm not like their grandma, so I would probably interrupt and give my advice or thoughts on the matter. I told them, "I give you permission to stop me from talking and interrupting them. Remind me to just listen because you need to vent, and I need to listen attentively." My children still remind me not to interrupt, and I'm so thankful!

Lord, you blessed me with a humble and loving mom! I will never forget her wisdom by example.

Show others, you value them by listening attentively.
Later on, share your thoughts.

Reflections:

- Are you quick to give advice, or are you listening to that person and understanding the person's feelings?
- It's never too late to start showing the person you value them by listening attentively.

God Wants You to Be

"To the elders among you, I appeal as a fellow elder and a witness of Christ's sufferings who also will share in the glory to be revealed: Be shepherds of God's flock that is under your care, watching over them—not because you must, but because you are willing, as God wants you to be; not pursuing dishonest gain, but eager to serve; not lording it over those entrusted to you, but being examples to the flock. And when the Chief Shepherd appears, you will receive the crown of glory that will never fade away" (1 Peter 5:1-4, NIV).

What do you notice?

The second part of verse 2 stands out to me. It says, *"...not because you must, but because you are willing, <u>as God wants you to be</u>..."* (emphasis added).

Lately, you've been telling me that you created me for a particular purpose. That's why you equipped me with specific characteristics or qualities.

Yes, I created each person uniquely for specific purposes. I want each person to *flourish* with the *potential* I give them. Like the verse says, "...as God wants you to be...". This is what *I want you to do!*

I'm slowly learning and understanding some parts, but I don't know what you mean by "with the potential" you gave me and others.

Like you said earlier, I have given you specific characteristics and qualities that make you unique. Those qualities are in you, but you're not using them to glorify me. That's why I said the potential

is in you. It's waiting to grow. When you use those qualities in my name, they flourish!

So, when I genuinely surrender and follow you, then the potential you gave me will come out and blossom! It will only grow because of the Holy Spirit and not because of what I'm doing. If it did, then I would take credit for it, huh?

Yes, now you're understanding. It's like creating this devotion book. I gave you the qualities of openness, straight-up honesty, boldness, compassion, talking, and listening to me. Like you stated in the introduction, you never thought I would ask you to write a book because you don't like writing. So, you know, putting this book together is not because you're a fantastic writer.

That's so true, Lord! I'm not fond of writing, but I do love talking.

I know. That's why this booklet is a collection of our conversations instead of essays.

Every time you created a new devotion, I was always shocked and blessed by what you said or told me to write. It's your wisdom, not mine.

Yes, these devotions are coming together because of *me*. The Holy Spirit guides you and tells you what words to write as you seek and listen to me. I'm also providing you with supportive friends to help you. So, I'd like *you* to share these quiet times that we've had together. When you first accepted me as your Savior, you came to me with child-like faith. You continue to do this, even as you get older. I always love this about you. I cherish the talks we have together!

Now, do you understand that you've always had these qualities I gave you? You're using those qualities to create a devotion book. I want everyone to know how much I love them! All I want is to sit and talk with them. I want to have a relationship with them as we do.

I understand, Lord. I want everyone to know and love you too, God! I don't know what I'd do without you in my life. You give me strength and peace and joy!

Lord, is this the only specific purpose I'm to fulfill?

Oh no! You've fulfilled many purposes in the past that pleased me and brought me great joy! Each person has many specific purposes, not one purpose. You have many more ahead of you too! Whenever you fulfill one of these purposes for me, you will receive absolute joy!

Yes, Lord! You're right! I can recall other times when I've been your vessel to help others. Now I understand more. I used the potential you gave me and fulfilled your specific purposes *(see devotions "Mustard Seed" and "Without Finding Fault").*

Yes! Please continue to fulfill my purposes with the potential or qualities I gave you.

Please help me to live my life to fulfill the purposes that are ahead! I want your potential in me to flourish and follow verse 2, "*Be shepherds of God's flock that is under your care, watching over them—not because you must, but because you are willing, as God wants you to be; not pursuing dishonest gain, but eager to serve*" (1 Peter 5:2, NIV, emphasis added).

Reflections:

- How are you using God's potential or qualities he gave you to fulfill his purposes?

Ephesians 2:10 (NIV), *"For we are God's handiwork, created in Christ Jesus to do good works, which God prepared in advance for us to do."*

God Shows Favor to the Humble

"In the same way, you who are younger, submit yourselves to your elders. All of you, clothe yourselves with humility toward one another, because, 'God opposes the proud but shows favor to the humble" (1 Peter 5:5, NIV).

I love humility, the humble servant. I dislike the proud or arrogant person.

I know, but that describes me. Of course, I try not to show it, but I can be a very arrogant or prideful person in my head.

Yes, I know.

As I look back on my life, I remember wanting certain things and telling you how my life should be. Man, I can't believe how ignorant I was when I was younger. Now, my faith is slowly maturing. Now I understand that you know what's best for me. You didn't give me the things I wanted or asked for back then because you knew they would make me even more prideful. You knew I already had some issues with pride. Thank you, Lord, for protecting me from the pain of having my way and keeping a lid on my pridefulness.

Yes, if you got what you wanted, you would have hurt your family! And that pain would have been unbearable because your family is so important to you!

Thank you, Lord, for your protection. Especially when I don't understand and when I grumble! You know what's best for me and everyone I love.

Show me when I'm proud, so I will ask you and others to forgive me.

I will show you, so keep an open heart. As we're writing this devotion book, I'm pleased that you're listening and have an open heart. In your introduction, you explained the beginning of this journey. Now I want you to include the rest of our conversation.

I understand. You had all of this planned out! That's so cool, Lord!

(Here's the rest of our conversation...)

There's one more thing you need to know. I don't want you to write your name as the author. It's not for privacy matters. It's to protect your pride issues. Do you understand what I'm saying?

Yes, I do, Lord. You know me so well. The enemy would slip in slowly and make me feel proud and take all the credit for creating this devotion book. Thank you, Lord, for protecting me. I understand, but how do I sign it? Do I make up a name?

I don't want you to make up a name. I want you to sign it as "H.S." This represents Humble Servant because that's what you are. I'm so pleased that you're being an obedient and humble servant as we go on this journey together.

I love that!

H.S. also represents Holy Spirit!

I love that even more, Lord! Yes! The Holy Spirit guides me. You're right! He's the actual author! Now I'm getting excited, Lord! You're amazing. This conversation started with a scared and nervous feeling, but you changed it into a positive one! I see a new and glorious adventure ahead. I'm not afraid anymore. How do you do that? Lord, you are so mighty, powerful, and love me! Thank you, Lord!

Reflections:

- Are you taking credit for your accomplishments? Or are you thanking God because he gave you outstanding qualities and strengths that you can use for his glory?
- How can you be God's Humble Servant?

Start Your Spark

Hey God,

I can't believe we're almost finished with the devotion book. You are amazing, Lord! Thank you, Holy Spirit, for your guidance and words! This has been an exciting and enlightening journey. You have taught me so much. I've learned the most important thing is to truly accept myself, especially my weaknesses. You keep telling me that you don't view my traits as weaknesses, but I do. You have shown me how you used my weaknesses in various ways to help others *(see devotions "Mustard Seed," "Good & Faithful Servant," "Without Finding Fault," and "God Wants You to Be")*.

I'm slowly understanding and appreciating that my weaknesses are also my strengths when I rely on you, Lord. My prayer is that everyone understands the words you gave me; recognize and use God's potential in each of us.

Yes, I understand how you feel. Your heart is overflowing with love for them. Here's another example I want you to share with everyone because some are confused with the phrase "God's Potential."

A match has certain chemicals inside it to make it ignite. Those chemicals are always inside that match. Once ignited, it can light a candle, which gives more light to show you the way. Or that little lit match can start a fire to create warmth for others. Either way, the match is fulfilled because it's doing what it was designed to do. The match can't be a straw. It can try, but it won't be fulfilled because it wasn't created to be a straw but a match.

Wow, that's cool, Lord. I like that analogy! I'm the match! You have given me certain quality traits that have always been in me. I can use them to do something positive and help others. You gave me those traits so I could live my life for you. "God's potential" is in me. They were there the day I was born. But I have to decide to use that potential you gave me. It's like how the Holy Spirit prompted me to write this devotional book together with you. Even though I didn't feel confident as a writer, I did what you said. The trait of talking openly or being transparent was there when I was born. Thank you, Lord and Holy Spirit, for guiding me and blessing me with these devotions.

Yes. I created you in a specific way to fulfill specific purposes that will give you peace and fulfillment. Writing the devotions has given you a more profound peace and joy. However, that match can also burn buildings down and cause people to die. So it has the potential to be a destructive tool also. If that match chose to destroy, it could. It wouldn't have inner peace and true fulfillment.

Yup, that's me too! Oh man, Lord! I become that destructive match when I'm focusing on myself and being selfish. I hurt others and get upset at myself. I definitely don't have inner peace during those times.

It's my choice to live for myself or live for you as you *created me to live*. Like the match, I can burn to give warmth or burn to destroy.

That match can also lie on the ground and do nothing. It will get trampled on by people walking on it. It still contains those unique chemicals I gave it, but it's not using them. Don't let that be you. Be a little spark to light the way for many people. Just start your spark!

I love that phrase, "Start Your Spark!" It's like that song, "Pass It On" by Kurt Kaiser.

It only takes a spark to get a fire going,
And soon all those around can warm up in its glowing;
That's how it is with God's Love,
Once you've experienced it,
You spread the love to everyone
You want to pass it on.

I wish for you, my friend
This happiness that I've found;
You can depend on Him.
It matters not where you're bound,
I'll shout it from the mountain top
PRAISE GOD!
I want the world to know.
The Lord of love has come to me.
I want to pass it on.

My prayer for everyone is that they live their lives with God's potential that's inside of them. Only then will they truly experience inner peace and joy!

Yes, be the match that glows and gives light to others and warmth of support!

Dear Friend,
You're saying, okay, but how do I do that?

First, you must "Accept Christ" and say a prayer. God doesn't care what words you say. He's more concerned about your heart's attitude. He knows what you mean and how you feel. You can say something like this.

Dear Lord Jesus,

I know I am a sinner, and I ask you for your forgiveness. Thank you for dying on the cross to pay the penalty for all my sins. Right now, I turn from my sins and open the door of my heart and life to you. Please come into my life and become my personal Lord and Savior. Thank you, Lord. Amen

Or if you accepted Christ a while ago and feel you've gone astray, then say a prayer of recommitment to God. It can be something like this.

Dear Lord Jesus,

I want to know the real YOU in all your glory. I want to have a close relationship with You. I've wandered away from You and have become lukewarm in my walk of faith. I'm sorry for not giving you total control of my life. Jesus, please forgive me. I come to you and recommit my life to you, Lord. May the Holy Spirit fill me so that I can listen to his whispers as he guides me and comforts me. Thank you, Lord, for always loving me! Amen.

Or you want to know God more by reading the Bible. Sometimes it's hard to understand. Just start small by meeting with God and talking with him. Then every day, read a section or chapter in one of the gospels (Matthew, Mark, Luke, or John), which describes the life of Jesus. Many Christians use the "S-O-A-P" method when reading the Bible.

S – Scripture	O – Observations	A – Application	P – Pray

There are numerous resources online with the SOAP example. They provide guiding questions to help you think. You can also join a Bible Study or meet with a fellow Christian brother or sister to help you.

Reflections:

- It's time for you to "make a decision." Reread this and decide.

My Simple Tips of Walking with God

Daily surrender your heart to God.

James 4:7 (NIV) "Submit yourselves, then, to God. Resist the devil, and he will flee from you."

Matthew 6:33 (NIV) "But seek first his kingdom and his righteousness, and all these things will be given to you as well."

Be honest with God; be transparent!

Psalms 51:10 (NIV) "Create in me a pure heart, O God, and renew a steadfast spirit within me."

Psalms 51:17 (NLT) "The sacrifice you desire is a broken spirit. You will not reject a broken and repentant heart, O God."

Focus on who God is—his character and his promises.

John 3:16 (NIV) "For God so loved the world that he gave his one and only Son, that whoever believes in him shall not perish but have eternal life."

Psalms 18:30 (NIV) "As for God, his way is perfect: The Lord's word is flawless; he shields all who take refuge in him."

Psalms 116:5 (NIV) "The Lord is gracious and righteous; our God is full of compassion."

Everyone wants to be loved and accepted
for who they are
ONLY GOD can give you that
pure and honest love!

Lord, I'm not in charge of the results,
but in charge of my obedience!

Dear Friend

Thank you for setting aside time to read this devotional book. As I listened to the Holy Spirit and wrote our conversations down, my prayer was that God would touch your heart, and you would feel his love. He loves you so much!

My son shared this with me: What does God consider to be a "Good Christian"? People will probably say, "reading the Bible," "going to church," "giving money," "being a good person," and so on. These are all good things in God's eyes.

But to God, the most important thing to him is: *having a relationship with him.*

I was amazed at my son's wisdom from God! He's right! So, start talking with God. You will see and understand how powerful talking with Him can be! God is waiting for you and ready to listen to you. He loves you!

My love and prayers are with you,
Humble Servant

CPSIA information can be obtained
at www.ICGtesting.com
Printed in the USA
BVHW052225220922
647830BV00005B/44